From the mid-1960s onwards Michel Foucault has had a significant impact on diverse aspects of culture, knowledge and arts including architecture and its critical discourse. The implications for architecture have been wide-ranging. His archaeological and genealogical approaches to knowledge have transformed architectural history and theory, while his attitude to arts and aesthetics led to a renewed focus on the avant-garde.

Prepared by an architect, this book offers an excellent entry point into the remarkable work of Michel Foucault, and provides a focused introduction suitable for architects, urban designers, and students of architecture.

Foucault's crucial juxtaposition of space, knowledge and power has unlocked novel spatial possibilities for thinking about design in architecture and urbanism. While the philosopher's ultimate attention on the issues of body and sexuality has defined our understanding of the possibilities and limits of human condition and its relation to architecture.

The book concentrates on a number of historical and theoretical issues often addressed by Foucault that have been grouped under the themes of archaeology, enclosure, bodies, spatiality and aesthetics in order to examine and demonstrate their relevancy for architectural knowledge, its history and its practice.

**Gordana Fontana-Giusti** is an architect, theorist and professor of architecture at the University of Kent, UK. She has taught at the Architectural Association, London and conducted research at Central Saint Martins College, London. Fontana-Giusti is the co-author of *Complete Works of Zaha Hadid* 4.vols. (Thames and Hudson, 2004) and *Scale: Imagination, Perception and Practice in Architecture* (Routledge, 2011).

# Thinkers for Architects

Series Editor: Adam Sharr, Newcastle University, UK

**Editorial Board**

Jonathan A. Hale, University of Nottingham, UK

Hilde Heynen, KU Leuven, Netherlands

David Leatherbarrow, University of Pennsylvania, USA

Architects have often looked to philosophers and theorists from beyond the discipline for design inspiration or in search of a critical framework for practice. This original series offers quick, clear introductions to key thinkers who have written about architecture and whose work can yield insights for designers.

> 'Each unintimidatingly slim book makes sense of the subjects' complex theories.'
>
> > Building Design

> '... a valuable addition to any studio space or computer lab.'
>
> > Architectural Record

> '... a creditable attempt to present their subjects in a useful way.'
>
> > Architectural Review

**Deleuze and Guattari for Architects**
Andrew Ballantyne

**Heidegger for Architects**
Adam Sharr

**Irigaray for Architects**
Peg Rawes

**Bhabha for Architects**
Felipe Hernández

**Bourdieu for Architects**
Helena Webster

**Benjamin for Architects**
Brian Elliott

**Derrida for Architects**
Richard Coyne

**Gadamer for Architects**
Paul Kidder

**Goodman for Architects**
Remei Capdevila Werning

**Foucault for Architects**
Gordana Fontana-Giusti

# Foucault

## for

## Architects

## Gordana Fontana-Giusti

Routledge
Taylor & Francis Group

LONDON AND NEW YORK

First published 2013
by Routledge
2 Park Square, Milton Park, Abingdon, Oxon OX14 4RN

Simultaneously published in the USA and Canada
by Routledge
711 Third Avenue, New York, NY 10017

*Routledge is an imprint of the Taylor & Francis Group, an informa business*

*British Library Cataloguing in Publication Data*
A catalogue record for this book is available from the British Library

*Library of Congress Cataloging in Publication Data*
Fontana-Giusti, Gordana.
Foucault for architects / Gordana Fontana-Giusti.
pages cm. -- (Thinkers for architects)
Includes index.
1. Foucault, Michel, 1926-1984. 2. Architecture--Philosophy. I. Title.
B2430.F724F584 2013
720.1--dc23
2013001756

ISBN: 978-0-415-69330-1 (hbk)
ISBN: 978-0-415-69331-8 (pbk)
ISBN: 978-0-203-74386-7 (ebk)

Typeset in Frutiger and Galliard
by Fakenham Prepress Solutions, Fakenham, Norfolk NR21 8NN

# Contents

# Series Editor's Preface

**Adam Sharr**

Architects have often looked to thinkers in philosophy and theory for design ideas, or in search of a critical framework for practice. Yet architects and students of architecture can struggle to navigate thinkers' writings. It can be daunting to approach original texts with little appreciation of their contexts. And existing introductions seldom explore architectural material in any detail. This original series offers clear, quick and accurate introductions to key thinkers who have written about architecture. Each book summarises what a thinker has to offer for architects. It locates their architectural thinking in the body of their work, introduces significant books and essays, helps decode terms and provides quick reference for further reading. If you find philosophical and theoretical writing about architecture difficult, or just don't know where to begin, this series will be indispensable.

Books in the Thinkers for Architects series come out of architecture. They pursue architectural modes of understanding, aiming to introduce a thinker to an architectural audience. Each thinker has a unique and distinctive ethos, and the structure of each book derives from the character at its focus. The thinkers explored are prodigious writers and any short introduction can only address a fraction of their work. Each author – an architect or an architectural critic – has focused on a selection of a thinker's writings which they judge most relevant to designers and interpreters of architecture. Inevitably, much will be left out. These books will be the first point of reference, rather than the last word, about a particular thinker for architects. It is hoped that they will encourage you to read further, offering an incentive to delve deeper into the original writings of a particular thinker.

The Thinkers for Architects series has proved highly successful, expanding now to nine volumes dealing with familiar cultural figures whose writings have influenced architectural designers, critics and commentators in distinctive and important ways. Books explore the work of: Gilles Deleuze and Felix Guattari; Martin Heidegger; Luce Irigaray; Homi Bhabha; Pierre Bourdieu; Walter Benjamin; Jacques Derrida; Hans-Georg Gadamer and Michael Foucault. A number of future volumes are projected, addressing Nelson Goodman, Jean Baudrillard and Maurice Merleau-Ponty. The series continues to expand, addressing an increasingly rich diversity of contemporary thinkers who have something to say to architects.

**Adam Sharr** is Professor of Architecture at the University of Newcastle upon-Tyne, Principal of Adam Sharr Architects and Editor (with Richard Weston) of *arq: Architectural Research Quarterly*, a Cambridge University Press international architecture journal. His books published by Routledge include *Heidegger for Architects* and *Reading Architecture and Culture*.

# Acknowledgements

I am thankful to Adam Sharr, the series editor, for his valuable comments and suggestions, Fran Ford and Georgina Johnson for their generous support from Routledge, and to Laura Williamson for her editorial assistance. I also wish to thank Marina Lathouri for her support in the early stages of this proposal, Megan Kerr for her reading of the final draft and Ranieri and Sofia for their reading of the drafts in-between. I remain indebted to Mark Cousins and the late Paul Q. Hirst for their interpretations of Foucault's ideas that have informed me throughout the years and to Bernard Tschumi for the discussion on events and cities in the final stages of writing this book. I am also grateful to the late Bogdan Bogdanović who argued about the importance of architectural knowledge and to the late Roy Landau whose masterminding of the History and Theory programme at the Architectural Association (AA) Graduate School was essential for my studies. I have benefited from numerous students and colleagues with whom I have exchanged ideas at the Architectural Association, Central Saint Martins College of Arts and at the University of Kent, whose questions and interests have supported me in this project. I need to extend my gratitude to the Head of Kent School of Architecture Don Gray and to the Dean of Humanities Karl Leydecker for the term off that helped the preparation of the initial manuscript.

## Illustration credits

Uppsala – Foucault, permission copyright: Association pour le Centre Michel Foucault, Paris.
Jackson Pollock, photograph by the author.
'Event', photographs by the author.
*Madness and Civilisation*, permission by the anonymous collector.
Foucault et Bernard-Henri Lévy, photograph by Michel Boncillon, permission copyright: Association pour le Centre Michel Foucault, Paris.

Michel Foucault lecturing, photograph by Michel Boncillon. Permission copyright: Association pour le Centre Michel Foucault, Paris.
Foucault's house, photograph and permission by Francesco Fontana-Giusti.
Foucault several weeks before his death, photograph by Michel Boncillon. Permission copyright: Association pour le Centre Michel Foucault, Paris.

# Introduction

One of the questions addressed repeatedly by the French philosopher Michel Foucault (1926–84) was, What is knowledge? *Qu'est-ce que le savoir?*

Is this question relevant for architects and if so, how? In order to comment on this and other Foucauldian enquiries of architectural significance this book asks what the position of Foucault's work is in relation to architecture, its knowledge, its design practice, its history and theory, and its criticism.

The book examines Foucault's project by focusing on selected aspects of his philosophy and by commenting on the works of architectural discourse and practice that have emerged in relation to his critical history of thought. The book thus opens up a territory where Foucault's discourse and architecture intersect or emerge in parallel. Due to its concise format, the book has had to be selective from its outset. The task has not been eased by the scope and range of Foucauldian scholarship and the knowledge of how Foucault marvelled in extended arguments and references collected from obscure sources.

Further challenges arose as the book takes Foucault's statements out of their original context in order to cross-examine them for the benefit of architectural knowledge. This kind of intervention could be justified by the philosopher's own approach to critical activity, where concepts are seen as tools. As Foucault's notions often slide, move and develop, refusing to stay in the same fixed place, this book remains vigilant as the ground covered by the dynamism of his thought becomes itself an interesting territory for architectural discussion.

This kind of thinking is part of Foucault's problem-centred discourse, which refuses to be translated safely into a set of applicable rules. Foucault's texts do not provide a 'solid foundation'; they work as an open archaeological and genealogical site where new questions and problems emerge (Cousins and

Houssain 1984). *Foucault for Architects* articulates the architecturally relevant notions and configurations that thus come to light.

The attitude of constant questioning and formulation of problems has been a part of Foucault's intellectual journey. Throughout his career, he tried not to 'interpret' but rather to produce 'commentaries' through which he constantly questioned, twisted and turned his thought. By adding new theoretical propositions along the way, his thought has changed internally (During 1992: 6). This agility of thinking, which steers the space of reflection, continues to keep Foucault's work alive, original and appealing to architects among others.

The attitude of constant questioning and formulation of problems has been a part of Foucault's intellectual journey. Throughout his career, he tried not to 'interpret' but rather to produce 'commentaries' through which he constantly questioned, twisted and turned his thought. By adding new theoretical propositions along the way, his thought has changed internally.

*Foucault for Architects* does not seek to be biographical, although the relevance of certain places (*lieux*), cities and architectural settings in Foucault's life will be mentioned as a logical extension of the discussion that will provide a better understanding of spaces, arguments and thoughts.

Foucault's summary of his own opus provided the initial, organisational structure for the book (Foucault 1998: 459–63). Here he related that by thought, he meant the act that determines and positions a subject, an object and their possible relations. By critical history of thought he understood an analysis of the conditions under which the positioning of a subject to object is formed, when they come to constitute knowledge (1998: 462).

By critical history of thought he understood an analysis of the conditions under which the positioning of a subject to object is formed, when they come to constitute knowledge.

This book follows the succinct format of the books in this series. It re-evaluates Foucault's discourse from a contemporary point of view by going beyond the popular perception that sees Foucault's contribution to architectural knowledge solely within the domain of the architecture of enclosures, prisons, hospitals and asylums. Such interpretation would prevent us from understanding the wider architectural implications of Foucault's project. This book thus points towards a broader spectrum of Foucault's ideas, manifested in the discussion about knowledge, archaeologies, bodies, urban space, aesthetics and spatiality.

The first chapter, Positioning, addresses Foucault's context by giving an outline of his contemporaries, significant events, his own position and approaches to the debates of the time. The two following chapters correspond to Foucault's two main streams of analysis.

The second chapter, Archaeology, addresses the conditions of the person who thinks (the knowing subject) and determines what Foucault thought the subject must be: what status he or she ought to have in order to become the legitimate subject of knowledge. This chapter relates to Foucault's *Order of Things* and *The Archaeology of Knowledge*. The examples of related architectural works are dealt with in the latter part.

The third chapter, Enclosure, addresses the objects of knowledge by considering the conditions under which something can become an object of knowledge – in particular, within the practices of psychiatry, clinical medicine and penality, where men and women have been the objects of Foucault's enquiry. The emergence of the 'great confinement' and the rise of the asylum, the clinic and the prison are discussed together with the role of the gaze and its functioning as the mechanism of control (*dispositif*), discipline and knowledge. Elaborated in *Discipline and Punish*, these instances mark Foucault's shift to 'genealogical' approach to history. A selection of the works by architects and critics who have made reference to this discourse concludes this chapter.

The fourth chapter, Bodies, addresses the question of sexuality within the discussion about the subject as an object of knowledge for himself or herself. The scope includes the questions of the techniques of the self, the truth and aspects of life in antiquity and Christianity, leading to a discussion regarding 'biopower' and urban societies. The chapter concludes with reference to the works of architectural critics and theorists that have scrutinised this area of Foucault's enquiry.

The fifth chapter, Spatiality / Aesthetics, analyses selected aspects of Foucault's discourse on aesthetics, space and spatiality. By focusing on the questions about the dynamics of Foucault's thinking, I have speculated on the ways in which Foucault developed an original and vivacious discourse that continues to captivate the minds of his readers. This thinking constantly calls for an examination of the space of discourse in which seeing, surface and three-dimensional transcendental experience all have a role.

By focusing on the questions about the dynamics of Foucault's thinking, I have speculated on the ways in which Foucault developed an original and vivacious discourse that continues to captivate the minds of his readers. This thinking constantly calls for an examination of the space of discourse in which seeing, surface and three-dimensional transcendental experience all have a role.

# CHAPTER 1

# Positioning

## 1.1 Context

Foucault was a thinker with wide academic interests that spanned from philosophy to psychology and further into the history of science. He read histories of medical and social sciences and his passion was linked to literary and political discourse. This made him a unique thinker whose work was at the time bridging unusually between separate aspects of life, knowledge and art.

Paul-Michel Foucault was born on 15 October 1926 in Poitiers, where his early years were marked by war, psychological difficulties and certain eccentricities, yet intellectually, he excelled from a young age. Having moved to Paris in 1946 to study at the École Normale Supérieure, rue d'Ulm, Foucault encountered the philosophies of Hegel and Marx. In the École, Hegel was studied with great attention through the work of Jean Hyppolite (1907–68) and Marx through the reading of Louis Althusser (1918–90). Both of these made a strong impression on Foucault. His two early works, 'Introduction' to *Dream and Existence* by Ludwig Binswanger and *Mental Illness and Psychology* were written in 1954 in response to this context. At the time, the phenomenologist of perception Maurice Merleau-Ponty (1908–61), who was linked to Jean-Paul Sartre, also taught here in rue d'Ulm.

Sartre (1905–80) had no direct sway on Foucault. Nevertheless, the thought of Sartre, as the thinker who marked the French philosophical and existentialist scene in the 1960s, persisted throughout most of Foucault's life. Foucault shared with Sartre a dislike of bourgeois society and a sympathy for groups perceived as being at the margins: artists, prisoners and homosexuals. Philosophically, Foucault rejected what he saw as Sartre's emphasis on the subject ('transcendental narcissism' as he called it), thus discarding Sartre's role as the 'universal intellectual'. When asked to comment on Sartre and the difference between Foucault's generation and that of his predecessor, Foucault stressed the importance of his generation's discovery of 'the eagerness for concepts' and above all for 'systems', and the departure from the idea of 'meaning' (*Quinzaine litteraire* 15 April 1966).

Central to Foucault's enthusiasm and appreciation for systems was the emergence of Claude Lévi-Strauss's work, namely *La pensée sauvage* (1962), dispelling all previous myths about meaning. According to Foucault, Lévi-Strauss demonstrated about societies what Lacan demonstrated in relation to the unconscious – that 'meaning' was

> a sort of *surface effect*, a shimmer, a foam, and that what ran through us, underlay us, and what was before us, what sustained us in time and space, was the system (*Quinzaine litteraire* 15 April 1966).

This system mentioned here by Foucault implies the idea of a spatial distribution, as every system is spatially organised. Foucault drew parallels between Lévi-Strauss and Lacan, leading him to point out the relevance of Lacan's work in determining the relationship between structures and systems of language. The French psychoanalyst Lacan argued that what spoke through the patient and his neurosis was not the subject but the acquired system of language, leading Foucault to state that 'before any human existence, there would already be a discursive knowledge, a system that we will rediscover' (Eribon 1993: 161). This system of language, which Foucault identified as discursive knowledge, was thus acknowledged as primary. For Foucault, the underlying system thus came first, while our process of the discovery of a discursive knowledge is a consequential result.

Foucault's work benefited from Georges Canguilhem's contribution to the history and philosophy of science. Canguilhem (1904–95) was Foucault's mentor and the supervisor of his doctoral thesis on the history of madness. He remained one of Foucault's most important lifelong supporters. Canguilhem's critical studies of biology provided a model for what Foucault was to achieve in the history of human sciences. Based on the work of Gaston Bachelard,

Canguilhem's approach gave Foucault a sense of the discontinuities and ruptures of science and an understanding of the historical role of concepts as independent of comprehension based on appearances. Canghuilhem's discourse revealed the inconsistencies of scientific knowledge and critically reviewed the role of concepts, showing evidence that concepts are determined by the conditions of a particular historic period. This approach remained central to Foucault, who reinforced it by deploying the linguistics and psychoanalysis developed by Ferdinand de Saussure and Jacques Lacan respectively.

## Based on the work of Gaston Bachelard, Canguilhem's approach gave Foucault a sense of the discontinuities and ruptures of science and an understanding of the historical role of concepts as independent of comprehension based on appearances.

On a different level, Foucault was fascinated by French avant-garde literature and art, especially by the works of Georges Bataille, Maurice Blanchot, Antonin Artaud, Jean Genet and Pierre Klossowski (Foucault 1977). Here, Foucault found concrete examples of the experiential and existential concerns in their most direct appearance. He was particularly interested in the 'liminal experiences' of human behaviour, where the usual categories of intelligibility begin to fall apart. This suggested to Foucault the review of concepts and knowledge from another angle – from a different set of experiences.

These diverse intellectual, artistic and literary milieus provided the background for the critical history of thought and the 'archaeological' and 'genealogical' approaches deployed in Foucault's historical critiques. His first major work was *Madness and Civilisation* (1961), which originated in the study of psychology and in visiting St Anne, a mental hospital in Paris linked to Lacan. Written during Foucault's post-graduate years (1955–9) while he held a series of diplomatic and educational posts in Sweden, Poland and Germany, *Madness and Civilisation* is a study of the emergence of the concept of 'mental illness'

Uppsala – Foucault sitting at the table in his apartment.

in Europe at the end of the eighteenth century. Foucault made a case against the irrefutable scientific truth of the time that madness was a mental illness. His second book, *The Birth of the Clinic* (1963), continued this questioning by critically addressing the emergence of clinical practice in the late-eighteenth and early-nineteenth century.

Following the publication of these books, Foucault became established; he maintained a number of academic positions at French universities throughout the 1960s and gained widespread recognition after the success of *The Order of Things* (1966), which made him a household name and an iconic figure in France. *The Archaeology of Knowledge* (1969), written during Foucault's stay in Tunisia, followed. Written as a methodological exposé, the book articulates the implicit historical approach ('archaeology') used in *Madness and Civilisation*, *The Birth of the Clinic* and *The Order of Things*. In the same year, Foucault was elected to the prestigious Collège de France, where he was the Professor of the History of Systems of Thought until his death.

Foucault was politically engaged at different points in his life. His early involvement with the political establishment started with the 1963 Commission that led to the reforms by the Ministry of Education in 1965. Foucault's assistance responded to the state's need for an activist intellectual to take part in the reforms and the students' needs for an academic who could articulate their discontent about the discrepancy between the elite *Grandes Écoles* and the universities of mass education. He became increasingly politically active in the 1970s, aiming to materialise some of his more radical ideas.

Foucault's reputation amongst his peers was at best ambiguous. He enjoyed respect and friendship from some colleagues, whilst others held him in suspicion. His eccentricity, plus his resistance to abiding by the rules and conforming to the fixed boundaries of disciplines and practices, contributed to this perception.

Foucault's activism after the demonstrations of 1968 is characterised by the disrupted relations between the state and intellectuals, particularly in establishing the new university at Vincennes. This period included stand-offs with the government and physical encounters with the police (Eribon 1993: 201–11). Foucault's role was to propose new academic staff and he took this as a chance to alter the French intellectual scene. Well-known successful candidates proposed by Foucault included Michel Serres, Judith Miller, Alan Badiou and Gilles Deleuze, who joined after Foucault's departure (Eribon 1993: 203).

Foucault's role was to propose new academic staff and he took this as a chance to alter the French intellectual scene. Well-known successful candidates proposed by Foucault included Michel Serres, Judith Miller, Alan Badiou and Gilles Deleuze, who joined after Foucault's departure.

Foucault was a founder of the *Groupe d'information sur les prisons* (Prison Information Group) and protested on behalf of marginalised groups. His *Discipline and Punish* (1975), a genealogical study of modern imprisonment, was set in opposition to torture or killing. While acknowledging the element of improvement, Foucault's book emphasised how such reform became a means of more effective discipline and how this new mode of punishment became the model for control of an entire society, including factories and hospitals. Foucault's dual concept of 'power / knowledge' showed that at least for the study of human beings, the goals of power and the goals of knowledge cannot be separated.

Foucault lectured outside France, in Europe, Japan and the United States, including regular teaching at the University of California, Berkeley. His final works arose from the exploration of the ancient world that he undertook later on in life while researching the history of sexuality. *The History of Sexuality* had been planned as a multi-volume work. The first volume, *Introduction*, came out in 1976 as *Volonté de savoir* (Foucault 1987a), while the planned second volume, *The Confessions of the Flesh*, has never been published. *The Use of Pleasure* and *The Care of the Self* (Volumes 2 and 3) appeared instead in 1984 (Foucault 1987b and 1990).

In parallel with the last two books of *The History of Sexuality*, the nature of Foucault's political involvement had changed. He became interested in the possibility of the state playing a specific role in promoting people's happiness. This kind of thinking involved themes centred on the manner in which individuals form themselves and focused on the investigation of the aspects of freedom and the self. The reasons for this turn and redirection of Foucault's discourse were many, including the time spent at Berkeley. California was a place in a series of 'other places' such as Uppsala, Warsaw, Hamburg and Tunisia that acted as catalysts for his work.

The initial support that Foucault had in 1981 for the French Socialist party in government was short-lived. He proclaimed his dissatisfaction with the government's lack of consideration for the problem of prisons (*Revue de l'Université Bruxelles* 113, 1984: 37). The ineffectiveness of political action resulted in his renewed interest in aesthetics and in a further exploration of the concept of self. Suffering from AIDS, Foucault died in Paris on 25 June 1984.

His lectures at the Collège de France were published posthumously, containing important clarifications and additions to his ideas.

Foucault remained a scientific realist in the tradition of his teacher Georges Canguilhem, despite his interest in the historical background and the social consequences of all truth-claims. Foucault wrote in appreciation of Canguilhem:

> ... in the history of science one cannot take truth as given, but neither can one do without a relation to the truth and to the opposition of the true and the false. It is this reference to the order of the true and the false which gives to that history its specificity and its importance (1985a: 3).

Foucault was therefore a rationalist and, when he discusses such notions related to the field of scientificity, he remains within the tradition of the French philosophers from August Comte (1798–1857) via Pierre Duhem (1861–1916) to Gaston Bachelard (1884–1962) and Louis Althusser (1918–90).

Michel Foucault was both an academic and a marginal. He was able to hold a prestigious chair at the Collège de France while having a life story that included a suicide attempt, breakdowns, a short period of institutionalisation, a police file and an early death. He was a human rights activist and a person able to shout misogynist remarks. Highly political and profoundly private, he was a dandy who managed to project the two contrasting aspects of his existence. In the words of Dumézil, one of his closest colleagues, Michel Foucault wore many masks (Eribon 1993).

Highly political and profoundly private, he was a dandy who managed to project the two contrasting aspects of his existence. In the words of Dumézil, one of his closest colleagues, Michel Foucault wore many masks.

This complexity, which appears as a reconciliation of the 'academic' and the 'transgressive', was not easy to bear. Foucault was initially troubled with his sexuality and kept his private life to himself. He never reflected in public about the change of institutional relations to which his work contributed, despite having played an important role in the transformation of perception and attitudes regarding madness, prisons and sexuality (Eribon 1993: 154).

## 1.2 Resisting boundaries

Part of the fascination with Foucault's work has been his resistance to disciplinary boundaries. His discourse was driven by its own logic, without concerns for the limits of usual subject areas, resisting the established interpretational procedures through which the books of philosophy had traditionally acquired their status. Even if we may have become used to interdisciplinary studies today, Foucault's skills in moving effortlessly and impeccably between disciplines and themes is exemplary.

This opening was possible because Foucault's ideas did not operate within the traditional intellectual context. He argued with precision, often pushing the point into a direction that would become irresistible to collocutors such as Georges Dumézil, Jean Hyppolite, Jules Vuillemin and Fernand Braudel (Eribon 1993: 61–98).

Foucault maintained that there were no longer assumed methodologies and approaches that were proper for certain subjects of investigation. The 'unproblematic parcelling out' of modes of thought was no longer sustainable; he considered the sense of security easily achieved by following the methodological path presumed right to be intellectually naïve. He argued that history needed to be approached as a category that required constant watchfulness, with theoretical attention to its methodologies and to the results it created and disseminated (Cousins 1989: 126–39). This would apply equally to the methods, approaches and effects of the history of architecture.

Foucault maintained that there were no longer assumed methodologies and approaches that were proper for certain subjects of investigation. The 'unproblematic parcelling out' of modes of thought was no longer sustainable; he considered the sense of security easily achieved by following the methodological path presumed right to be intellectually naïve.

The shift in human sciences from the eighteenth century onwards as demonstrated by Foucault was characteristic of many disciplines, including architecture. Architectural knowledge in France in the late-eighteenth and early-nineteenth century became rationalised, thus losing many of its transcending characteristics. Despite excellent contributions to the subject, such as the critical history of eighteenth-century French architecture by Anthony Vidler (1988 and 2011), architecture's discourse can still expand further in the area of critical revision of the architectural canon and the norms in urban policies.

## 1.3 Architecture unspoken

Foucault's questions in respect to architecture and urbanism open up on various levels: on the level of knowledge / discourse and discursive practice; on the level of architectural effects upon social relations; on the level of body politics and 'biopower' (Foucault's term for the techniques for achieving the subjugations of bodies and the control of population); and on the level of aesthetics and spatiality.

His discourse is also significant in the critical approach to the profession itself. He analysed the nature of professions, the language they create, the schools they constitute and the institutional structures that they form in order to further their cause within society. In this way, he argued, professions have been able to maintain their status and their exclusivity.

Having shown that terms such as 'society', 'equality' and 'liberty' went through a form of identity crisis from which architecture was not exempt, Foucault reminds us that architects need to remain critical, as they have at different times and to various degrees been involved in the processes that have set up, determined or overthrown people's liberties. We are not to forget that architecture interferes with people's lives, the way people use and occupy space, as well as with the individual sense of the aesthetico-ethical categories such as beauty and propriety.

In the age of digitalisation and global networks, architectural institutions are again in the process of self-examination. Despite appearances, new conditions of communication that have replaced the traditional systems are not apolitical or equally open to all. At a time when representational democracy, government and governability are being marginalised by the global financial world that escapes public scrutiny or electoral responsibility, there is a renewed interest in the analyses of Michel Foucault. It could mean asking questions such as these: what are the underlining conditions that determine knowledge and relations of power today? How did these new phenomena emerge? What has changed and what has remained the same in the process of digitalisation, instant messaging and exposure to global access? Moreover, can the epistemological openings proposed by Foucault translate into discursive and spatial categories that will continue to challenge the entrenched positions of all those who are too comfortable under the status quo – bureaucrats, bankers, developers, managers, architects, academics, and so on? Can these openings lead us to an architecture that conditions a more fulfilled, good and happy life in the space that is yet to be imagined and a discourse that still needs to be announced?

At a time when representational democracy, government and governability are being marginalised by the global financial world that escapes public scrutiny or electoral responsibility, there is a renewed interest in the analyses of Michel Foucault.

It could mean asking questions such as these: what are
the underlining conditions that determine knowledge and
relations of power today?

In his essay 'Space, Knowledge and Power', Foucault explained how he
understood architecture 'as an element of support, to ensure a certain
allocation of people in space, a *canalization* of their circulation, as well as the
coding of their reciprocal relations' (1991b: 239–57). He thus maintained that
spatial effects determine social relations.

Foucault explained how he understood architecture 'as an
element of support, to ensure a certain allocation of people in
space, a *canalization* of their circulation, as well as the coding
of their reciprocal relations'.

Foucault's knowledge of architecture and its history was generally restricted
to the French context. In his archaeology of human sciences, he refers
only to Vitruvius's treatise, conspicuously omitting reference to a series of
fifteenth- and sixteenth-century Florentine and Venetian treatises. At the
same time, it is the French context that made Foucault's project possible,
as the embodiment of social relations of both power and knowledge was
most prominent there.

At the same time, it is the French context that made Foucault's
project possible, as the embodiment of social relations of both
power and knowledge was most prominent there.

Foucault refers to eighteenth-century and later French sources, as he identifies the realm of urban planning and government (*police*) to be the channels in the distribution of power, leading him to perceive the architect's role as limited in the overall societal context of power relations. According to Foucault, architects are not as powerful as doctors, psychiatrists, judges or prison wardens. He believed, perhaps somewhat optimistically, that individuals were still in charge of their own space and that architects were not able to impose and determine the space of individual dwellings, implying that private dwellings are the ultimate places of resistance.

In a further blow to the architects' sense of self-importance, Foucault argued that there was no such thing as an architecture of freedom, since liberation was something to be lived, practised and striven for. Despite architects' claims of commitment to freedom, Foucault believed that freedom was not a property of any architectural object or space. He was conversant with Le Corbusier and the Modern movement and he regarded the criticism of Le Corbusier at the time as exaggerated and unfair, stating that the pioneer of Modern architecture was treated as a 'crypto-Stalinist'. In respect to the 1980s modernism / postmodernism debate, Foucault's attitude was balanced, showing clear understanding and sympathy towards the position of rationality in defending Modernism (1991b: 245–9). Foucault has always been radically against any form of historicism (i.e. forms of thinking that assign a central significance to a historical period, geographical place or a culture), which he often ridiculed.

He was conversant with Le Corbusier and the Modern

movement and he regarded the criticism of Le Corbusier at

the time as exaggerated and unfair, stating that the pioneer

of Modern architecture was treated as a 'crypto-Stalinist'. In

respect to the 1980s modernism / postmodernism debate,

# Foucault's attitude was balanced, showing clear understanding and sympathy towards the position of rationality in defending Modernism.

At another level it is important to stress that Foucault's thought almost organically embraces space and different spatial categories. It is not simply that his thinking about psychiatric knowledge comes with the notion of the asylum or that his studies about the history of medicine or punishment involve the space of the clinic or that of the prison; Foucault's thinking is always clearly spatially articulated. This way of thinking contains at least three different spatial modes: a) spatial metaphors – mainly in early essays; b) space and architecture as the model for the spatiality of thought – predominantly in *The Order of Things* and *The Archaeology of Knowledge*; and c) architecture as the extension of the discourses and practices within society – as in *Madness and Civilisation*, *The Birth of the Clinic* and *Discipline and Punish*.

Commitment to his own radical thinking, which was an implicit personal methodology, meant that Foucault opened up his critical discourse in a different space, thus unlocking the discourse on power. The release coming from this opening was proportionate to the scale of previous suppressions. From Foucault's point of view, the past and the present were put under the spotlight, presenting what went before in an entirely different manner on the level of knowing, understanding and morality.

Foucault advocated that his arguments should be used in challenging, analysing and dismantling the relations of power and oppression in society. The possibility of understanding how our knowledge relies upon its underlying and determining structures ultimately depends upon our ability to liberate thought and ourselves in the context. For various reasons this deliverance is not easily achieved. Foucault called for renewed self-reflection within any discipline constructing itself as knowledge.

Foucault advocated that his arguments should be used in challenging, analysing and dismantling the relations of power and oppression in society. The possibility of understanding how our knowledge relies upon its underlying and determining structures ultimately depends upon our ability to liberate thought and ourselves in the context.

On a societal level, Foucault examined the grounds of democracy by stating that Enlightenment categories such as 'equality' or 'justice' failed to truly reach the people, due to the technologies of social administration that have become detached from the political apparatus established during the time of the revolutions, whose developed form is modern representative democracy. Thus, according to Foucault, almost invisibly, power and politics have become disjointed (Donzelot 1979; Pasquino 1978; and Rajchman 1985).

Not unrelated is Foucault's answer to the question he was often asked: what is the philosopher's role in society? His answer was:

> Philosophers do not have a role in society. Their thought cannot be situated in relation to the current movement of a group. Socrates is an excellent example: Athenian society could see him only as subversive, because the questions he raised were not acceptable to the established order. In reality, a philosopher's role is acknowledged only after a certain period of time; it is in short, a retrospective role (Carrette, ed. 1999: 85).

In reality, a philosopher's role is acknowledged only after a certain period of time; it is in short, a retrospective role.

This was followed by another question: how then do you integrate yourself into society?

> Integrate myself...? You know, until the nineteenth century, philosophers were not recognised. Descartes was a mathematician, and Kant did not teach philosophy, he taught anthropology and geography; you learned rhetoric, not philosophy, and so there was no need for philosophers to be 'integrated'... (1999: 85).

When contemplating the shifting position of the disciplines, Foucault identified the changes that occurred in the role of the humanities, as they have ceased to possess the emancipatory and transcending power they once had as liberal arts. Instead, they have gradually become another form of training or a means of transmitting cultural capital. We can halt here by putting the same commentary to architecture. Is architecture potentially on course to undermine itself as knowledge and become another form of training in the service of the economy?

Foucault identified the changes that occurred in the role of the humanities, as they have ceased to possess the emancipatory and transcending power they once had as liberal arts. Instead, they have gradually become another form of training or a means of transmitting cultural capital. We can halt here by putting the same commentary to architecture. Is architecture potentially on course to undermine itself as knowledge and become another form of training in the service of the economy?

# CHAPTER 2

# Archaeology

## 2.1 Human sciences, knowledge and architecture

Foucault's investigation of the emergence of human sciences in *The Order of Things: An Archaeology of the Human Sciences* has been ground-breaking and widely persuasive. In the foreword of the English edition (1970), he points out that this book addresses a neglected field, as the history of science traditionally discusses the rigorous sciences of mathematics, cosmology and physics, in whose history one can observe 'the almost uninterrupted emergence of truth and pure reason' (1991: ix). Other disciplines, those concerning human beings, languages or economy, have been considered too exposed to the vagueness of empirical thought, chance, imagery or tradition to be considered sciences and as such to have a history of relevance to knowledge. It is this empirical, non-exact and uncertain kind of knowledge based on evidence of unstable discourses – such as the state of mind, intellectual fashions, combination of archaisms, conjecture and intuition – that he writes about in *The Order of Things*.

Other disciplines, those concerning human beings, languages or economy, have been considered too exposed to the vagueness of empirical thought, chance, imagery or tradition to be considered sciences and as such to have a history of relevance to knowledge.

Although Foucault does not refer to architecture specifically, we sense how architectural knowledge – which is a complex blend of learning containing a variety of practical, scientific and aesthetic skills – fits this category. This multifaceted mixture of architectural knowledge has at different times been organised according to different sets of rules. The perceived condition of 'lack of order' and volatile empirical knowledge that apparently characterised the architectural treatises of the fifteenth and sixteenth century became a problem. This led Marc-Antoine Laugier (1713–69) and other learned individuals of this period to attempt to put it right in their own writings. From the eighteenth century onwards, constant resetting of architectural knowledge has been part of the architects' debate.

In the archaeology of human sciences, Foucault therefore asked a crucial question: 'what if empirical knowledge, at a given time, and in a given culture, *did* possess a well-defined regularity?' (1991: ix) In *The Order of Things*, this question unfolds into an elaboration on three analyses of knowledge presented in parallel: analysis of the laws of language, of living beings, and of economic facts, covering the time period from the seventeenth until the twentieth century. This work is not just about studying a particular period, i.e. it is not identifying a particular symptom of the time. *The Order of Things* is a comparative study: it investigates and compares various occurrences in unison. It not only discloses the root causes of the phenomena related to language, studies of living beings or economy, but observes and examines the laws of these phenomena in comparison, in order to state a critical point about the underlying knowledge at the time.

*The Order of Things* is a comparative study: it investigates and compares various occurrences in unison. It not only discloses the root causes of the phenomena related to language, studies of living beings or economy, but observes and examines the laws of these phenomena in comparison, in order to state a critical point about the underlying knowledge at the time.

Foucault has established that every historical period is characterised by a fundamental paradigm (understood as a particular standard) which delineates the cultural production of specific types of knowledge – the *episteme*. Episteme is shared by all knowledge and is the implied precondition that determines and makes it possible for all related discourses or works to emerge. Foucault refutes approaches by the traditional history of science that addressed this issue by relying upon notions such as 'the influences'. He does not see this new category as a missing content that needs to be restored. Rather, he aims to reveal a different, *positive unconscious* of knowledge, one that makes knowledge possible – one that requires human imagination to think of its possibility.

Foucault refutes approaches by the traditional history of science that addressed this issue by relying upon notions such as 'the influences'. He does not see this new category as a missing content that needs to be restored. Rather, he aims to reveal a different, *positive unconscious* of knowledge, one that makes knowledge possible – one that requires human imagination to think of its possibility.

By elaborating on the episteme, Foucault intended to restore that specific *experience* of a culture, which is situated between culture's own ordering codes and our reflections upon this order. He called this experience the 'pure experience of order' (Foucault 1991: xxi). This aspect of his approach is often neglected in scholarship, such as architectural history, which frequently approaches the archives without questioning their ordering codes and our perception of them.

The intricacy of this kind of thinking is expressed in the preface of *The Order of Things*, which has a paragraph from Borges quoting a 'certain Chinese encyclopaedia' and its peculiar division of animals (Foucault 1991: xv). In reading this now (in)famous classification, our mind is trapped struggling with the twists and turns of the configuration of this classificatory thinking. As disparate notions can't be conceived because they do not share the common ground (or plane of intersection of any kind) between themselves and with our modes of thinking, they remain suspended in separate spaces. In acknowledging the importance of the 'ground' as an empty and 'mute' field upon which the concepts could be placed, Foucault has effectively shown the spatial mechanism that is involved in 'making' thought and which depends upon this shared plane of consistency (Foucault 1991: xvii).

### *Las Meninas, resemblances and representation*

*The Order of Things* is famously prefaced by 'Las Meninas', a pictorial first chapter that was reportedly Foucault's afterthought (Eribon 1993: 155). While the book's layered argument spanning over four centuries holds neatly without it, 'Las Meninas' equips the book with an example that illustrates the change of the dominant episteme in European culture. This, I will show, indicates the change from the realm ruled by resemblances into the era of representation. Because the painting Las Meninas by Diego Velázquez (1599–1660) emerged at this critical point in time, when the roles of language and of visual demonstration were altering on a larger scale, Foucault was driven to analyse this picture in depth. His aim was to ascertain not simply the portrayal of the room in the palace of Philip IV, but likewise to determine the underlying conditions of the broader episteme lying beneath life, the relationships of power and the role of art. Thus Foucault's analysis of Velázquez's 1656 masterpiece examines the enigmatic arrangements of the painting's overall composition, its sight lines, foreground / background dichotomy, positions of various characters and their appearance – in the mirror, in the painting or both. He explores the canvas's convolutedness and the multi-focal arrangement that creates an uncertain relationship between the viewer and the figures depicted.

Thus Foucault's analysis of Velázquez's 1656 masterpiece examines the enigmatic arrangements of the painting's overall composition, its sight lines, foreground / background dichotomy, positions of various characters and their appearance – in the mirror, in the painting or both.

Foucault states that Las Meninas is the painting that neatly shows the complexity of 'painterly representation'. He argues that Velázquez leaves the spectator's attention suspended, because 'the entire painting is looking out at a scene for which it is itself a scene, a condition of pure reciprocity...'. (Foucault 1991: 14). As a result, it is not clear who or what is the exact subject of the painting: the king and the queen, whose reflections are in the mirror and to whom the painter is oriented, or the central group of characters around the young princess, or the painter in the act of painting. In respect to this changing position of the subject(s), Foucault suggests that:

> ... in the midst of this dispersion which is simultaneously grouping together and spreading out before us, indicated compellingly from every side, is an essential void; the necessary disappearance of that which is its foundation – of the person it resembles and the person in whose eyes it is only a resemblance (1991: 16).

Indeed, if we compare this setup with the fifteenth-century viewer's position, the conditions are different. There we had the theme of the painting (Alberti's *istoria* – usually a biblical story) clearly presented for the subject to view, read and contemplate. In the situation of Las Meninas, argues Foucault, the position of the subject has been disturbed and ultimately omitted, paving the way for the representation to be freed from the relation that was previously holding it back. Representation can now offer itself in its pure form. What was holding it back

In the situation of Las Meninas, argues Foucault, the position of the subject has been disturbed and ultimately omitted, paving the way for the representation to be freed from the relation that was previously holding it back.

before was the late-medieval and sixteenth-century structure of thought that had established itself through the dominant system of resemblances. This system was bound to the subject interpreting the signs that were clear only to those who could recognise them. In this way, this kind of thinking was bound by the subject and depended upon subject's knowledge, perception and imagination. The representation as it emerged in the middle of the seventeenth century is no longer based on this dependency and limitation. The image becomes more explicit, skilful and unwavering, and thus gradually independent of the subject.

The representation as it emerged in the middle of the seventeenth century is no longer based on this dependency and limitation. The image becomes more explicit, skilful and unwavering, and thus gradually independent of the subject.

This phenomenon worked in parallel with the circulation of seventeenth-century knowledge centred on the proliferation of illustrated printed material. Think of the translations of books with images such as those by Palladio and Vignola spreading around the major cities of Europe. They are noticeably different from the manuscripts such as Alberti's De re aedificatoria that were circulated in the fifteenth century without illustrations. Velázquez's talent was to sense this moment of change and to express it in his picture. He did so by revealing the picture's ordering system to the viewers.

Foucault wrote about Velazquez's Las Meninas in order to analyse the conditions of painting, its size, its spatial arrangement, its framing as well as the set of power relations in relation to the viewer. We can analyse the same and other conditions in this situation where viewers look at a painting by Jackson Pollock.

This point was raised in the book on the origins of perspective by Hubert Damisch, who refers to Foucault from the outset, pointing out his contribution to 'the vastness of the heuristic power of perspective and its value as a model for thought that continues to exercise its influence over the widest range of domains' (Damisch 1995: xiii). Damisch concludes that Foucault's 'Las Meninas' has been immensely successful in originating a philosophical discourse with never-ending susceptibilities (1995: 425–6). Quoting Leo Steinberg, he states that any descriptions of Velazquez's masterpiece must remain inadequate and incomplete, as Las Meninas has become a work of art of a status that is comparable to a piece of music lending itself to multiple commentaries that cannot ever be exhausted (Steinberg 1981: 45–54). This is an important tribute to the achievement and impact of Foucault's theoretical and cultural analysis of this painting.

Following 'Las Meninas' is an astonishing chapter entitled 'The Prose of the World'. Here Foucault goes back in time to describe the fifteenth and sixteenth centuries' system of resemblances, their underlining episteme and its role in the formulation of the perception of the world. His explanations are detailed; his archival material is delivered with passion. The reader feels party to an extremely unusual moment in the history of human knowledge, as Foucault explains how similitudes and resemblance guided the writing and the interpretation of texts and events for centuries. Resemblances (the four most prolific being the *convenientia, aemulatio, analogy* and *sympathy*) did so by acting as an omnipresent, invisible thread that organised the play of symbols and supplied the general framework for knowledge. In this way, Foucault argues, by wrapping up aspects of life and knowledge, the unified idea of the world was maintained.

The reader feels party to an extremely unusual moment in the history of human knowledge, as Foucault explains how similitudes and resemblance guided the writing and the interpretation of texts and events for centuries. Resemblances (the four most prolific being the *convenientia, aemulatio, analogy* and *sympathy*) did so by acting as an omnipresent, invisible thread that organised the play of symbols and supplied the general framework for knowledge.

These explanations of the realm of resemblances and the emergence of representation are highly original, truthful and penetrating. Still, unlike some other better-known aspects of Foucault's work that have been incorporated into contemporary discourses, this shift in discourse has not yet been fully appreciated. This is because we have departed from the realm of resemblances long ago without effectively leaving access to this knowledge. In that sense, after a lengthy period of time in the history of

European thought, Foucault's archaeological approach was able to unearth this point of entry to the previous way of thinking by means of grasping the mechanisms of its systems of knowledge. We find it difficult to grasp, because Foucault unlocked the thinking whose understanding has been hindered and unavailable for centuries. He thus awoke the thoughts that lay dormant within the ancient volumes of texts and rekindled the possibility of understanding the world as the *scaena mundi* – 'the world stage' – once again (Foucault 1991: 17).

In that sense, after a lengthy period of time in the history of European thought, Foucault's archaeological approach was able to unearth this point of entry to the previous way of thinking by means of grasping the mechanisms of its systems of knowledge.

In organising this scene of historical investigation, Foucault provided guidance for understanding sixteenth-century texts and artefacts. By bringing the forgotten discourses to the fore, Foucault has opened up the dialogue between (previously) cryptic treatises, their precedents in Antiquity and our reading of these texts today. It was Foucault who explained how Antiquity was perceived as a vast space with signs to be discovered, and how prophecy (*divinatio*) and erudition (*eruditio*) had been parts of the same system of thinking (1991: 33–4). In attending to these arguments, Foucault articulated the nature of the epistemological gap left by the legacy of the eighteenth century. He thus provided the missing lines of reasoning in the history of Western thought, which is why this book was a major success when it appeared.

In attending to these arguments, Foucault articulated the nature of the epistemological gap left by the legacy of the eighteenth century. He thus provided the missing lines of

## reasoning in the history of Western thought, which is why this book was a major success when it appeared.

In showing the order in comparative developments of language, natural creatures and economic exchanges, which includes the emergence and workings of the category of representation, *The Order of Things* outlines the way in which culture made the existence of this order manifest. This order has had its parallel development in arts and architecture. Recent art and architectural critical theory became involved in addressing its implications.

In *The Grid Book* (2009), Hannah Higgins presents a compendium of intersecting discourses that inform the reader about the historical conditions that came to determine the understanding and usage of notions such as the 'grid' by focusing on ten grids: the brick, the tablet, the gridiron city plan, the map, musical notation, the ledger, the screen, moveable type, the manufactured box and the net. Higgins thus addresses the manifold ways in which the notion of the grid was deployed by attending to a form of archaeology. In providing the critical background for her commentaries, she refers to Foucault's discourse on knowledge, which she defines as 'a communicator of the social flow of the society' (Higgins 2009: 185). Echoing *The Order of Things* throughout the book, Higgins argues that the grid of the screen of perspectival painting heralded the science of the modern period, classical mechanics and the screen arts (2009: 189).

### *Ruptures and epistemes*

Foucault's archaeology of human science has identified two great ruptures in the history of European knowledge: one that emerged approximately in the middle of the seventeenth century, indicating the beginning of what he called the Classical Age (*l'âge classique*), and a second that emerged at the beginning of the nineteenth century, marking the start of the Modern Age.

These findings disturbed the perception of the continuity of a Western culture that apparently developed in a unified manner. The quasi-continuity on the level of ideas and themes is only 'a surface appearance' for Foucault, as the deeper archaeological investigation into the modalities of thinking, i.e. into *the governing episteme*, reveals a different logic. Therefore, the function of the episteme is of marking, establishing and mapping the undercurrents of general knowledge at a particular time and for a specific culture. Allied with archaeology, the episteme penetrates into the buried set of underlying possibilities that enabled thoughts to appear as valid statements. Foucault argues,

> ... one thing in any case is certain: *archaeology*, addressing itself to the *general space of knowledge*, to its *configurations*, and to the mode of being of the things that appear in it, defines systems of simultaneity, as well as the *series of mutations* necessary and sufficient to circumscribe the threshold of a new positivity (Foucault 1991: xxiii).

The quasi-continuity on the level of ideas and themes is only 'a surface appearance' for Foucault, as the deeper archaeological investigation into the modalities of thinking, i.e. into *the governing episteme*, reveals a different logic.

Foucault maintained that it is therefore possible to establish throughout the long eighteenth century a series of coherent relationships between thematically separate knowledge such as the theories of representation, of language, of the natural orders or of wealth and value. The discontinuity at the beginning of the nineteenth century meant that these types of knowledge, governed by representation, gradually ceased to exist, while new kinds of knowledge progressively emerged. This was possible only after the dissemination of detailed taxonomies that mapped, placed and represented the content of disciplines within a consistent plane. The best example is the Encyclopaedia by Diderot and d'Alembert.

Foucault maintained that it is therefore possible to establish throughout the long eighteenth century a series of coherent relationships between thematically separate knowledge such as the theories of representation, of language, of the natural orders or of wealth and value. The discontinuity at the beginning of the nineteenth century meant that these types of knowledge, governed by representation, gradually ceased to exist, while new kinds of knowledge progressively emerged.

The new knowledge that emerged in the nineteenth century gave rise to a profound preoccupation with historicity and to the forms of order implied by the continuity of time. Foucault argued that things thus became increasingly thought of in terms of their *internal* development (in time) and not as a *series* (in space). In this respect, the analysis of monetary exchange became political economy, the taxonomy of organisms was replaced by biology, and above all, argued Foucault, language lost its privileged position and was studied in philology as 'a historical form coherent with the density of its own past' (Foucault 1991: xxiii).

The new knowledge that emerged in the nineteenth century gave rise to a profound preoccupation with historicity and to the forms of order implied by the continuity of time. Foucault argued that things thus became increasingly thought of in terms of their *internal* development (in time) and not as a *series* (in space).

As the dominant principle of internal development observed through time took supremacy, it became noticeable in other disciplines such as chemistry, medicine and architecture. Previous architectural systems of thought based on taxonomy such as the one by Seroux d'Agincourt (1730–1814) were replaced by those tracing the origins of building and its structure internally. In the context of nineteenth-century architecture, the theoretical work by Gottfried Semper, *The Four Elements of Architecture* (1851), provides a good example. Here the origins of architecture are explained through the dominant principle of internal development of the four main elements: the hearth, the roof, the enclosure and the mound (Semper 1989).

This reflexivity driven by the exploration of the interiority (the inner structure) has increasingly involved the study of humans in the same way. Consequently, argued Foucault, man entered the field of knowledge as studies of human anatomy, evolution, human types and different racial developments led to the emergence of anthropology and psychology. At the same time, architectural knowledge explored buildings' interiority, leading to concerns about the structures and interiors of edifices. In relation to human dwellings, we observe increased interest in domestic interiors, paving the way for the modernist functional analysis of houses and ultimately for functionalism.

Man entered the field of knowledge as studies of human anatomy, evolution, human types and different racial developments led to the emergence of anthropology and psychology. At the same time, architectural knowledge explored buildings' interiority, leading to concerns about the structures and interiors of edifices. In relation to human dwellings, we observe increased interest in domestic interiors, paving the way for the modernist functional analysis of houses and ultimately for functionalism.

The place of the human became that of a subject who reflects and is at the same time subjected to reflection through the scientific disciplines that have established an unreserved confidence in this process of thinking. This recognition drove Foucault to argue that 'the human as known to us is a recent invention, a rift in the knowledge' in the *longue durée* scheme of things (in the long term). He added,

> It is comforting, however, and a source of profound relief to think that man is only a recent invention, a figure not yet two centuries old, a new wrinkle in our knowledge, and that he will disappear again as soon as that knowledge has discovered a new form (Foucault 1991: xxiii).

This statement, often quoted, which emerges rather surprisingly, disconnectedly and unexpectedly at the end of the introduction to *The Order of Things*, appears to have another startling capacity which prevents us from fully grasping its meaning. We are left suspended again as we are told that human existence as we know it is already on its way out.

The rupture foreseen by Foucault is perhaps already with us, as the centre of our investigations has started to shift from the human towards the environment, with direct implications for architecture.

## 2.2 Archaeology as difference

What can the archaeological approach offer architects that other methods of research cannot provide? Is archaeology different from the domain known as 'the history of ideas'? In elaborating on these questions in *The Archaeology of Knowledge*, Foucault outlines the crucial difference of his approach by making a number of suggestions.

They include a new, fresh examination of the past and its remains, which should be observed in an unprejudiced way as 'monuments'. This approach should be achieved from a certain exteriority. The monuments, according to Foucault, are not thoughts, representations, images or themes revealed in discourse, but rather they are seen as containing clear direct traces and imprints whose existence has not been thought yet.

Foucault supposed that this unbiased exteriority of thinking would in turn allow for new things to emerge and would not attempt to rediscover some continuity that constantly relates the existing discourses to each other. The emphasis is on the explorations of the specific conditions of possibility of any enterprise, be it in architecture or history of science. In that sense, he is not particularly interested in naming individuals or in dating the phenomena, but in finding out the conditions under which certain thoughts and practices are made possible (Foucault 1985: 136).

In that sense, he is not particularly interested in naming individuals or in dating the phenomena, but in finding out the conditions under which certain thoughts and practices are made possible.

In establishing an 'archaeology', Foucault was driven by a suspicion of power and of educational institutions' right to claim and interpret in the name of knowledge. From the same scepticism stems his unease with the idea of interpretation in general. According to Foucault, if interpretation can never be achieved, it is because there is nothing to interpret; it was always too late to uncover an 'original meaning' and a stable 'context', because 'everything has always already been only interpreted'. This condition has political and institutional consequences as it allows 'good researchers' within institutions to be privileged (Foucault 1971: 192–201).

According to Foucault, if interpretation can never be achieved, it is because there is nothing to interpret; it was always too late to uncover an 'original meaning' and a stable 'context', because 'everything has always already been only interpreted'.

This is why, through archaeologies, Foucault remained unrelenting in his will to demonstrate the conditions of knowledge, its emergence, its circulation and its effects on individuals, and to call for the next step:

> By going a little further in the same direction, and coming back, as if by a new turn in the spiral, just short of what I set out to do, I hoped to show the position from which I was speaking; the map of space that makes possible these investigations and others that I may never accomplish; in short, to give meaning to the word *archaeology*, which I had so far left empty (Foucault 1985: jacket).

For Foucault, this extended realm had fewer fixed boundaries, as boundaries by definition have always produced limited consideration, have reduced diversity of dialogues and have thrived upon exclusions. For political reasons, he is in favour of a world that has less fascination with 'aura' (understood in a general sense). Foucault believed that the captivation with concepts such as 'humanity', 'art' or 'architecture' served to obscure the relation between the individual and knowledge by means of the apparatuses that administer modern society. The relevance of this point has grown recently as modern societies (alarmingly including academia) have been administered with lesser concerns for the relationship between individuals and knowledge. Instead, in the societies of late capitalisms, the emphasis has been on knowledge that is relevant for performativity (Lyotard 1979).

For Foucault, this extended realm had fewer fixed boundaries, as boundaries by definition have always produced limited consideration, have reduced diversity of dialogues and have thrived upon exclusions.

## Statements, events, discursive formations

I shall now refer to the categories that are important for Foucault's archaeology of knowledge. The two that emerge most prominently are the categories of statement (*énoncé*) and event (*événement*). In brief, these two categories have maintained a direct link to a phenomenon that is being considered; as such, for Foucault these categories are as unmediated as they could be.

The two that emerge most prominently are the categories of statement (*énoncé*) and event (*événement*). In brief, these two categories have maintained a direct link to a phenomenon that is being considered; as such, for Foucault these categories are as unmediated as they could be.

Statement is considered to be a somewhat forgotten basic unit of discourse that enunciates and expresses an utterance or a proposition. As such, for Foucault, it has a primary function in any discourse. In order to release the language from complex narratives, Foucault argued that it was necessary to disengage the statements into their initial 'event' mode as they had 'originally irrupted' – i.e. as they had initially been stated. Foucault had thus opened up the way for statements to be rewritten into new unities of discourse. In elaborating on discursive formation, which forms part of his methodology, Foucault demonstrated the process of 'disengagement' and the conditions for potentially new discursive formations:

> Whenever one can describe, between a number of statements, such a system of dispersion, whenever, between objects, types of statement, concepts, or thematic choices, one can define a regularity (an order, correlations, positions, functionings and transformations), we will say, for the sake of convenience, that we are dealing with the *discursive formation* (Foucault 1985: 38).

Without giving concrete examples but rather speaking metaphorically, Foucault describes discourses as 'a work in progress', temporarily fixed 'intersections of things and words', a kind of 'web of language' that 'sits chained to the things'. He remains suspicious about any privileged and established form of discourse, as it limits the wider access and hinders the possibility of new thoughts emerging. By arguing that in critical analysis, one sees 'the loosening of the embrace' between words and things, and the emergence of rules proper to discursive practices, Foucault deploys an architectural metaphor:

> **Behind the visible facade of the system, one posits the rich uncertainty of disorder; and beneath the thin surface of discourse, the whole mass of a largely silent development [*devenir*]: a 'presystematic' that is not of the order of the system; a 'prediscursive' that belongs to an essential silence. Discourse and system produce each other (Foucault 1985: 76).**

Foucault describes discourses as 'a work in progress', temporarily fixed 'intersections of things and words', a kind of 'web of language' that 'sits chained to the things'. He remains suspicious about any privileged and established form of discourse, as it limits the wider access and hinders the possibility of new thoughts emerging.

We are led to think of how the façade of knowledge is a precarious layer and that the system is not absolute and robust but fragile and prone to changes. Foucault states that the 'thin surface' of discourse protects and moulds the system and that in this way discourse and system work together and produce each other.

Foucault argues against the unities that keep together the histories of ideas, of science or of knowledge. He attacks categories such as tradition, influence, development and evolution, because they enable the grouping of dispersed statements and events by linking them to the same organising principle. In this process, he argues, the statements flatten, and the dispersed events

> **become subjected to the exemplary power of life, to the principle of coherence, to the mastery of time through a perpetually reversible relation between an origin and a duration (Foucault 1985: 76).**

He attacks categories such as tradition, influence, development and evolution, because they enable the grouping of dispersed statements and events by linking them to the same organising principle.

The statements and the events thus lose their edge and authenticity – something they still had in the moment of their initial irruption. We know this is the case in any narration of events and replication of statements. In scholarship, it is evident in the use of the 'secondary sources', as they often involve generalisation, synthesis, interpretation or evaluation of the authentic information.

The statements and the events thus lose their edge and authenticity – something they still had in the moment of their initial irruption.

Foucault's term 'dispersion' indicates a particular kind of regularity whose configuration cannot be predicted, as it might involve different kinds of correlations, positions, functioning and transformation that go beyond the usual and expected understanding of identity and proximity. That is to say, if we are to embark on an investigation we need not worry about the nature and the extent of the elements and sources we might come upon and wish to deploy. They could be varied, dispersed, disjointed and significantly different in nature, size and modality. What they need to have in common is the regularity, yet to be discovered, which goes beyond the usual and the expected.

In his essay entitled 'De-, Dis-, Ex-' (1996), Bernard Tschumi acknowledges a parallel condition in architecture, arguing that the cities are the places of dispersion and disjunction of many often-invisible systems. He makes reference to Foucault in relation to what Tschumi calls the 'essential disjunction' that exists in the process of architectural production. Tschumi's continuing strategy has been to turn these dispersions and complexities into advantages. He argues that the architect's ability to see the underlying dispersions as new regularities of an urban context can contribute towards finding a new creative solution for a particular problem in urban design.

In his essay entitled 'De-, Dis-, Ex-', Bernard Tschumi acknowledges a parallel condition in architecture, arguing that the cities are the places of dispersion and disjunction of many often-invisible systems. He makes reference to Foucault in relation to what Tschumi calls the 'essential disjunction' that exists in the process of architectural production.

'Event' was an irreducible category for Foucault in *The Archaeology of Knowledge* and it features as one of the key concepts in Bernard Tschumi's project for Parc de la Villette.

Echoing Foucault's understanding of the event, Tschumi states that the category of *event* is an underscoring notion for architecture, as there is no architecture without programme, no programme without action and no action without event. For Tschumi, these phenomena are part of architecture, and architects need to engage on this level of analysis. He has dedicated four printed volumes of *Event-Cities* to this subject (2001; 2003; 2012).

'Event' continues to be important for Tschumi's thinking about cities – *Event-Cities 1–4* (1994–onwards).

## The category of *event* is an underscoring notion for architecture, as there is no architecture without programme, no programme without action and no action without event.

Importantly, Foucault argues that the paradigm of the 'spirit of the time' needs to be suspended, as it has been used to safeguard 'the community of meanings', the symbolic links and the interplay of resemblances that would otherwise be difficult to hold (1985: 76). He contends that we are always to question these 'ready-made syntheses' – the groupings that we tend to accept without examination such as the Renaissance or the Enlightenment.

For architect and historian Manfredo Tafuri, Foucault's critical analysis of past systems of thought was highly relevant. In *The Sphere and the Labyrinth*'s introductory essay, 'Historical Project' (1980; 1987), Tafuri discusses the questions of history and architecture. Alongside the critical approaches by Marx, Nietzsche, Benjamin and Adorno, Foucault is an important voice for Tafuri. In his books of architectural histories and theories, we can observe Tafuri's emphasis on statements of primary evidence and on the questioning of the presumed unities that is supported by Foucault's discourse. Tafuri's critique of historical periodisation, and his references to the notions of the 'sphere' and the 'labyrinth', make implied reference to Foucault's work.

### Dispersing the author and the oeuvre

As part of his constant attempt to demystify the 'creative subject', Foucault argues against the category of the 'author' and of the '*oeuvre*'. According to his argument, categories such as 'author' or 'oeuvre' create inappropriate (false) and misleading unities. Consequently, archaeology does not aim at restoring *the moment* in which the author and the *oeuvre* exchange identities.

According to his argument, categories such as 'author' or 'oeuvre' create inappropriate (false) and misleading unities. Consequently, archaeology does not aim at restoring *the moment* in which the author and the *oeuvre* exchange identities.

With respect to architectural history, theory and criticism, Foucault's work questions groupings and divisions with which we have become familiar. According to Foucault, we cannot always know for certain what exactly was meant by a certain term or a division. Furthermore, concepts such as 'architecture', 'literature' or 'politics' could only be conditionally applied to medieval culture or to classical antiquity, he argued, as none of the three would have articulated the same field of discourse and practice then as they do today. Foucault outlines the unities that must be suspended above all, including the book:

> ... the frontiers of a book are never clear-cut: beyond the title, the first lines, and the last full stop, beyond its internal configuration and its autonomous form, it is caught up in a system of references to other books, other texts, other sentences: it is a node within a *network* (Foucault 1985: 23).

The authorship of a building cannot be clearly defined either. A building is not a unity, but a particular dispersion indebted to other buildings, other architects and other builders. It is a 'node within the networks' of architecture and related discourses that are themselves diverse and grouped separately as functional, aesthetic, structural and signifying discourse.

The authorship of a building cannot be clearly defined either.
A building is not a unity, but a particular dispersion indebted
to other buildings, other architects and other builders.
It is a 'node within the networks' of architecture and
related discourses that are themselves diverse and grouped
separately as functional, aesthetic, structural and signifying
discourse.

The potential closure of the traditional understanding of the *oeuvre* in architecture should not be difficult to imagine, as it is indeed a reality in contemporary architectural practice. The attribution of the authorship of a building to a single person is an antiquated thing to do. However, this archaism is still present because our understanding of the role of the architect has been entrenched within the notion of *oeuvre* for too long, at least since Plato. Western culture's deep-rooted fantasy of an architect or creator of edifices still reigns, despite all the evidence to the contrary. With an understanding fostered by the media rather than reflecting on the true epistemological or practical conditions of architecture, our culture still names individual architects as mighty authors. The myth of an all-knowing architect, which has sustained itself from Antiquity, via Quattrocento treatise writers and the fathers of Modernism to contemporary architects, needs to be reviewed and suspended. This myth disseminates no knowledge and no truth about the building; it persuades through fantasy and a set of power relations established by the profession at different periods of time. More recently, it has been fuelled by the power of the broadcasting images disseminated and consumed in the culture of late capitalism.

The attribution of the authorship of a building to a single person is an antiquated thing to do. However, this archaism is still present because our understanding of the role of the architect has been entrenched within the notion of *oeuvre* for too long, at least since Plato.

In Foucault's understanding, the thought of an *oeuvre* as a property belonging to one person – the author – presupposes a number of choices that are 'difficult to justify or even formulate'. With respect to architecture, they may include the following. Where does the *oeuvre* of an architect begin and where does it end? What is the status of architectural drawings: should one count all the drawings and sketches, including those that the architect has abandoned? What about the fact that the work is delivered by many employed unnamed professionals? Do the laws of capitalism overturn the truth of authorship?

Where does the *oeuvre* of an architect begin and where does it end? What is the status of architectural drawings: should one count all the drawings and sketches, including those that the architect has abandoned? What about the fact that the work is delivered by many employed unnamed professionals?

There is a need to disperse the unquestioned continuities of the author and the *oeuvre* according to which architecture is organised before we attend to its critical analysis. Once the forms of presumed and unquestioned continuity between discourses are suspended, argues Foucault, an entire field becomes open. This is the field of 'effective statements' in their dispersion as events that provide for potential new unities (Foucault 1985: 79).

An example of this need for the dispersion of the existing continuities is the notion of the 'classical', as argued by Peter Eisenman in his article *The End of the Classical* (1984). Here Eisenman criticises the extended role of 'classical' architecture and its values since the Renaissance, suggesting the need to overcome it, as 'the classical' has been a dominant episteme that has underlined Western architecture for centuries, including through twentieth-century Modernism. Eisenman states that for the last five centuries, architecture has not achieved the 'radical break' from the classical episteme, despite the claims and appearances of the avant-garde. He proposes a fundamental disengagement of the language of architecture from the previous narratives and 'fictions' of the classical architecture. While Foucault's discourse helped Eisenman to formulate his own, it is important to point out that Eisenman does not use the term 'classical' in the same way as Foucault did.

Eisenman states that for the last five centuries, architecture has not achieved the 'radical break' from the classical episteme, despite the claims and appearances of the avant-garde. He proposes a fundamental disengagement of the language of architecture from the previous narratives and 'fictions' of the classical architecture.

*Events, objects and surfaces of emergence*

Before studying any work (be it a book or a building), the description of events needs to be established, Foucault states. The documentary material ought to be reduced to events, ideally presented in a neutral way. Foucault argues that we must show how and why the established events could not have happened in any other way. For example, the critic is not reporting on the recent 'exhibition on the work [*oeuvre*] of Leonardo' but on the 'events surrounding the exhibition of the paintings, drawings, sketches and notebooks attributed to Leonardo da Vinci'. The purpose is the suspension of accepted unities that prevent us from restoring the phenomenon to its original conditions of occurrence. The understanding of the process ultimately reveals how unities and discontinuities are accidental in their nature, 'not at all unlike the phenomena in geology' (Foucault 1985: 27). Indeed, many attributions of paintings and drawings to particular artists and architects deserve re-examination as new conditions of knowledge might provide different responses.

The understanding of the process ultimately reveals how unities and discontinuities are accidental in their nature, 'not at all unlike the phenomena in geology'.

Discursive events are comparable to design processes in architecture, in the way in which the 'dispersion of effective statements' is reminiscent of an architect's dispersion of sketches, drafts and outlines. One of the crucial moments in any enquiry is the naming of the objects of investigation. In architecture, this could be linked to the formulation of the design brief, as the initial naming of objects will define the design and the new set of relations. We are aware of winning competition entries where the successful architectural design proposal is the one that suspends the obvious understandings, breaks them into existing elements and disperses them in a new way, thus creating design beyond expectations.

One of the crucial moments in any enquiry is the naming of the objects of investigation. In architecture, this could be linked to the formulation of the design brief, as the initial naming of objects will define the design and the new set of relations.

Foucault focuses not solely upon the naming of objects but crucially on the surfaces upon which this emergence is mapped. It is through the initial processes of recording, charting, plotting and diagramming upon surfaces that objects of investigation come to life. This happens according to the degree of rationalisation, conceptual codes and types of theories that will be possible to contemplate.

This process might set into motion new surfaces of appearance while beginning to function with implications for spatial thinking and architectural space. Indeed, the architectural discourse and practices that involve the consideration of the field and make a so-called field design testify to the relevance of this point for architecture. Stan Allen, among others, has argued eloquently about the relevance of the surface of inscription in the formulation of an architectural field and has pursued this in his design work (Allen 1997: 24–31).

This process might set into motion new surfaces of appearance while beginning to function with implications for spatial thinking and architectural space.

Significantly, Foucault abandons efforts to see a discourse as a phenomenon of expression or interpretation of the previously established synthesis and narratives. Instead, he looks for the fields of regularity that determine the positions of subjectivity and discourse.

For example, Francoise Choay's *Rule and the Model* (1980; 1997) has questioned and dispersed previous boundaries that have structured knowledge of the Renaissance. By radically challenging the existing assumptions and dominant narratives, Choay scrupulously analyses the emergence and dissemination of the fifteenth- and sixteenth-century architecture, focusing on concepts such as the 'rule' and the 'model'. She demonstrates the relevance of these new foci by showing how Alberti and More's 'institutional texts' exhibit a formal 'regularity and stability' which identifies them as specific discourses; as such they were appropriate for her critical investigation (Choay 1997: 9).

### *Archives*

The archive is of relevance for Foucault as an instance in the process of making statements and of the articulation of discursive formations. It is not a simple repository; it is a place (*locus*) of a special kind where various groups of statements are differentiated in accordance with specific rules and practices.

Instead of the traditional archives that were 'the great mythical books of history', Foucault proposes what he calls 'density of discursive practices, systems that establish statements as events (with their own conditions and domain of appearance) and things (with their own possibility of use)' (Foucault 1985: 128). His insistence on the uniqueness of statements as events is here extended into the realm of discursive practices and things, where things are considered to be purposeful objects and practices intense activities all in need of consideration.

Foucault proposes to call these systems 'archives' and maintains that by this term he does not mean the sum of all the texts that a culture has kept as documents of its own past or as evidence of its continuous identity. Equally explicitly, he is uninterested in the institutions that make it possible to record and preserve those discourses that one wishes to remember and keep in circulation, such as museums and traditional archives. On the contrary, Foucault is interested in a new kind of archive because the old type was a problem. It privileged and perpetuated certain objects and discourses by means of its organisation, choice of documents, underpinning discourses, and so on. It was the obstacle and 'the reason why so many things, said by so many men, for so long, have not emerged' in accordance with their own laws of thought or set of circumstances (1985: 129).

Foucault is interested in a new kind of archive because the old type was a problem. It privileged and perpetuated certain objects and discourses by means of its organisation, choice of documents, underpinning discourses, and so on. It was the obstacle and 'the reason why so many things, said by so many men, for so long, have not emerged' in accordance with their own laws of thought or set of circumstances.

In this vein, Foucault states that archive is better served by 'grafting' original statements in a haphazard way than by subordinating them to another overall discourse which would be alien to the regularities that have borne them to life. He adds that an archive determines that things do not accumulate endlessly in an amorphous mass or an unbroken linearity, as they need to be grouped, allowing for the multiplicity of relations to be maintained or blurred according to specific rules. For example, when he was writing on the emergence of prisons in *Discipline and Punish*, Foucault had accumulated a large archive of historical material and documents from the eighteenth-century French context. However, he challenged the dominant idea that the prison came to life only due to humanitarian concerns of reformists. By following his heterogeneous archival material, he examined the details and traced the unaccounted shifts in culture that led to the emergence of prisons. Foucault's focusing on the body and questions of power became an important presupposition.

An archive is thus diverse and, according to Foucault's argument, can take various shapes and forms. It embodies and defines *the system of possibilities for statement or things to come to life*. The archive defines the mode of occurrence of the statement or of the discourse and, consequently, it defines knowledge. Foucault dissociates the archive from the notion of tradition, as his 'archive' does not have that traditional gravitas, nor does it stand for the central library beyond time and place. Foucault's archive is set between tradition and oblivion and enables statements to survive and modify (1985: 130).

It is impossible to capture the archive in its totality, as it emerges in fragments, in regions, and at different levels. We cannot describe our own archive, since it is from within these rules that we speak and since we use its depository for our statements.

> **The analysis of the archive, then, involves a privileged region: at once close to us, and different from our present existence, it is the border of time that surrounds our presence, which overhangs it, and which indicates it in its otherness; it is that which, outside ourselves delimits us (Foucault 1985: 130).**

The archive is that which gives us what we can say, draw, sketch or write; in that sense, it is an all-inclusive system. Foucault's archive is spatially set between the language that defines the system of constructing possible sentences and the physicality of the archive that passively collects the spoken words.

## Foucault's archive is spatially set between the language that defines the system of constructing possible sentences and the physicality of the archive that passively collects the spoken words.

At the same time, Foucault's archive is not just a passive collection of records from the past; it is an active and controlling system of enunciation (Foucault 1985: 129). The archive gives ever-changing form to the 'great murmur' that emanates from the discursive formation. The archive has a set of meanings (a 'form') that changes with the mental frame we bring to it. According to

Foucault, there is an active relationship between the archive, statements and discursive formations as he describes the archive acting on the statement (1985: 130).

Andrei Piotrowski's *Architecture of Thought* is indebted to Foucault's discourse on several levels. Indicating its own tone from the outset, the book opens up with Foucault's question: what does it mean not to be able to think a certain thought any longer? (Piotrowski 2011: 1) The text makes references to several Foucauldian notions and themes such as discursive formations, epistemological shifts in the constitution of knowledge in the eighteenth century ('*déblocage épistémologique*'), the production of reality and the technology of the observer (2011: 268). Pietrowski moves through different systems of thoughts, practices and archives, highlighting the hidden recesses of discourse and drawing our attention to the gaps in knowledge such as the architectural history of Byzantium, the colonization of Mezoamerica, the Reformation and Counter-Reformation in Eastern Europe and the effect of the rise of consumerist culture in Victorian England upon Modernism among others.

There is, therefore, a body of works by architectural historians, theoreticians and practitioners which has emerged in the last thirty years that makes reference to Foucault's seminal texts on the archaeology of knowledge and human sciences. In these works of architectural theory, Foucault's interdisciplinary approach, drawing on philosophy, history, literature, art and politics, has proven to be highly relevant. One of the profound, long-term effects of these texts has been evident in more thoughtful and nuanced approaches to architectural knowledge, its history and its theory. This chapter has demonstrated how Foucault's widespread intellectual and cultural input continues to impact architecture and how this is due to his penetrating, analytical and archaeological studies of knowledge.

CHAPTER 3

# Enclosure

## 3.1 Madness

*Madness and Civilisation* (1961) emerged as a response to Foucault's studies
of psychology and the history of psychiatry. The book is based on 21,000
documents, spanning from the sixteenth century to the beginning of the
twentieth century. It refers to a large archive of material acquired by the
library of Uppsala from a certain Dr Erik Waller that included a collection of
the doctor's own research into the history of medicine. The Swedish archive
was beneficial for Foucault and he explored it systematically (Eribon 1993: 83).
*Madness and Civilisation* is the outcome of this research but also of Foucault's
own experience and of suspicion towards modern psychiatry, which he saw as
a form of control that preserved conventional morality.

According to Foucault, the idea that the mad were 'mentally ill' and in need
of medical treatment was not an improvement on earlier attitudes such as the
sixteenth-century stance that the mad were possessed by mysterious forces,
or the eighteenth- and nineteenth-century view of madness as insanity. He
wrote:

> We have yet to write the history of that other form of madness, by
> which men, in an act of sovereign reason confine their neighbours, and
> communicate and recognise each other through the merciless language of
> non-madness (Foucault 2009: xi).

This discourse has had a radical reverberation ever since, as Foucault called for
the return to that neutral stance, a point zero at which madness is imagined as
an indistinguishable experience. Foucault aimed to evoke an understanding of
madness as a simple difference in behaviour or attitude, rather than a different
category that from the start dismisses the mad from the realm of reason and

/ or knowledge. In making this call, Foucault described the trajectory of the conditions that separated and positioned Reason and Madness as 'divided, deaf to all exchange, and as though dead to one another' (2009: xi). In pointing out this lack of dialogue and constructive discussion between the two, the book confronted, challenged and harnessed the attitudes and intellectual positions that later developed and justified some intrusive approaches in psychiatric therapy. The intrusive forms of therapy, such as electric shocks, were still practised at the time *Madness and Civilisation* was written. Foucault acknowledged that this is an 'uncomfortable region' of thought where in order to exploit it one must renounce the convenience of what one understands to be true, and never let oneself be guided by what we may already know about madness. He temporarily dismissed the existing concepts in psychopathology as unfit because the actions that have isolated madness from reason needed to be reviewed.

Foucault aimed to evoke an understanding of madness as a simple difference in behaviour or attitude, rather than a different category that from the start dismisses the mad from the realm of reason and / or knowledge.

### *Mental illness and environment*

In his *Mental Illness and Psychology* (1954), Foucault introduces the issues linked to his overall approach to mental illnesses and to psychoanalysis in particular:

> **Two questions present themselves: Under what conditions can one speak of illness in the psychological domain? What relations can one define between the facts of mental pathology and those of organic pathology? (Foucault 1987: 1)**

Foucault states that mental pathology requires methods of analysis different from those of organic pathology and that it is only by a trick and artfulness of language that the same meaning can be attributed to 'illness of the body' and 'illness of the mind' (1987: 10). For Foucault, aiming towards this new and different formulation of the discourse on mental pathology and madness includes the role of the arts. He often stated that to speak of madness one must have the talent of a poet (Eribon 1993: 70).

Foucault's approach to madness is multifaceted: it develops from several sources, which deserve mention. He builds upon the work of his teachers – Jean Hyppolite's theorising on alienation and environmental conditions, Georges Canghuilem's approach to the history of science and Jacques Lacan's post-Freudianism – as well as upon his own openness to the arts and the diverse experience of artists (see Chapter 1: Positioning). In the introduction to his doctoral thesis on madness, Foucault listed Lacan, Blanchot, Roussel and Dumezil as persons who inspired him, while the works of artists such as Hieronymus Bosch, Breughel and Goya continued to be present alongside contemporaries such as Artaud and Klossowski. The works of these artists and writers are often used as a reference that appears throughout Foucault's work (see Chapter 5: Spatiality / Aesthetics).

Since it appeared in 1961, *Madness and Civilisation* has prepared and inadvertently announced the scope of Foucault's subsequent work. The analysis of great confinements raised the questions of power, observation and surveillance, while the status of knowledge and language was mentioned through the critique of the broken dialogue between madness and reason. Foucault stated that he had not tried to write 'the history of this language' but 'rather the archaeology of this silence' (2009: xii). When making a point about the lack of dialogue, Foucault quotes infrequently heard statements that reflected on this condition, such as Pascal's uttering that men are so necessarily mad that not to be mad would constitute another kind of madness. Similarly, Foucault brings in a quotation from Dostoyevsky, who argued that it is not by confining one's neighbour that one is to be convinced of one's own sanity (2009: xi).

The analysis of great confinements raised the questions of power, observation and surveillance, while the status of knowledge and language was mentioned through the critique of the broken dialogue between madness and reason. Foucault stated that he had not tried to write 'the history of this language' but 'rather the archaeology of this silence'.

### Reason / Madness

Writing about this silence – this lack of dialogue between reason and madness – meant excavating Western culture that since the Middle Ages had established a relationship with something it called madness. Foucault points out how unsystematic and arbitrary this nature of the 'Reason–Madness' connection was. This polarity and the inconsistency in accounting for the relationship between the two parties has been a characteristic that constitutes one of the dimensions of European originality to which Western reason owes some of its depth. Foucault acknowledged that this originality and this ambiguity towards madness had accompanied Western culture long before Bosch and would follow it long after Nietzsche and Artaud (Foucault 2009: xiii).

The Reason–Madness relationship needs to question the assumed distance between the two and to address the subjugation of non-reason to reason, argues Foucault. In doing so, he describes the Reason–Madness relationship spatially, by introducing connotations linked to the geometrical concepts such as the 'horizontal course' and 'verticality'. Foucault asks,

> Where can an interrogation lead us which does not follow reason in its horizontal course, but seeks to retrace in time that constant verticality which confronts European culture with what it is not? What realm do we enter which is neither the history of knowledge, nor history itself? (2009: xiii)

Foucault contemplates this realm, which he states is controlled neither by the purposefulness of truth nor by the rational sequence of causes. He adds that causes here have value and meaning only beyond the established reason / madness division. Foucault sees this realm in need of restructuring and openness, where the previous questions about identities such as reason/ not-reason or mad/not-mad will be surpassed.

The main argument of *Madness and Civilisation* is structured around several historical events: 1) the emptying of *leprosaria* (leper asylums) at the end of the Middle Ages; 2) the foundation of Hôpital Général and the 'great confinement' in Paris in 1656; and 3) the 'liberation' of the mad at the end of the eighteenth century by Pinel in 1794. Foucault's 'classical period' thus covers the time between the creation of the Hôpital Général (1656) and the liberation of the chained inmates in Bicêtre (1794). According to Foucault, during this period the language between madness and reason was radically modified, as a new structure was formed which clarified and polarised the language. The main difference was that previously man's dispute with madness had been seen as a dramatic debate in which man confronted the secret powers of the world (2009: xiii–iv).

According to Foucault, during this period the language between madness and reason was radically modified, as a new structure was formed which clarified and polarised the language. The main difference was that previously man's dispute with madness had been seen as a dramatic debate in which man confronted the secret powers of the world.

This drama, continues Foucault, contrasts with our era 'where the experience of madness remains silent in the composure of a knowledge which, knowing too much about madness, forgets it' (2009: xiv). Foucault argues that there remains one vital task: 'to speak of the experience of madness', to rediscover it before its full takeover by knowledge and scientific discourse. Even more vitally, it is important to let madness express itself, to let it speak itself. Foucault adds urgency by saying that we need to define the moment of this conspiracy before it is permanently established in the realm of truth (2009: xi).

This drama, continues Foucault, contrasts with our era 'where the experience of madness remains silent in the composure of a knowledge which, knowing too much about madness, forgets it'.

If this warning was vitally important in 1961, suffice it to say that it is even more so today. We may mention an example in which madness shows its overwhelming richness and superiority. Japanese avant-garde artist Yayoi Kusama, who has recently exhibited in London and worldwide and who is by her own choice a permanent resident in a mental hospital, comes to mind. The recent encounter with Kusama's work in London has made us perceive and experience space which neither reason nor the most intricate computer programming could propose or configure. Kasuma's work (and shall we say, madness) raises questions in regards to the opening up of the space of infinity, perception of depth, limitless possibilities of individual projections and their relationship to the universe and universal. It shows a certain epistemological potency in madness that still needs to be grasped.

Kasuma's work (and shall we say, madness) raises questions in regards to the opening up of the space of infinity, perception of depth, limitless possibilities of individual projections and their relationship to the universe and universal.

## Spaces of exclusion and great confinements

Throughout *Madness and Civilisation*, Foucault moves from one register to another, analysing madness on various levels – economic, juridical, medical and artistic – maintaining the rigor and the radical tone of the discussion. His erudition and love for detail come through across various branches of history of knowledge. On an artistic and architectural level, the book is remarkably pictorial, as we are led to contemplate the sites such as the vacant and uninhabitable spaces that stretch over the wasteland of former *leprosaria* that were based at the edge of medieval cities throughout Europe. Images from Albrecht Dürer's engravings or more recently from Ingmar Bergman's *The Seventh Seal* (1957) come to mind. By quoting the primary sources (documents and monuments), Foucault provides statistical evidence about these spaces, stating that there were 19,000 lazar houses throughout Christendom around 1226; out of this, 2,000 were in France and 43 in Paris.

In *Madness and Civilisation* Foucault discusses the lepers and *leprosaria* as places at the edge of the cities. Here we see Albrecht Dürer's sixteenth century representation of the leper from the 'Passion' series.

On an artistic and architectural level, the book is remarkably
pictorial, as we are led to contemplate the sites such as
the vacant and uninhabitable spaces that stretch over the
wasteland of former *leprosaria* that were based at the edge
of medieval cities throughout Europe. Images from Albrecht
Dürer's engravings or more recently from Ingmar Bergman's
*The Seventh Seal* (1957) come to mind.

According to Foucault, England and Scotland in the twelfth century had
220 lazar houses for 1.5 million inhabitants suffering from leprosy and the
disease was almost eradicated by the end of the fourteenth century. The most
well-known sites included those in Ripon, St Albans, Romenal and Chatham
in Kent. The last one, St Bartholomew, Chatham, established in 1078, became
virtually empty at the time of Queen Elizabeth I and closed in 1627. Similar
examples from Germany are mentioned in relation to the cities of Leipzig,
Munich, Stuttgart and Hamburg (2009: 3). After the dissolution of the
*leprosaria*, the Royal authority and the French Parliament attached the lazar
houses to hospitals (c.1693–5).

Despite the closures, which were celebrated and welcomed, Foucault
argues that something of a permanent mark remained in the minds of
inhabitants of these cities – the values and images of exclusion, and the
social importance they acquired. These values were more difficult to erase
than leprosy. The leper disappeared, but the social structures of urban
experiences remained. Often in the same locations, 'the formulas of
exclusions will be repeated, strangely similar two or three hundred years
later' (Foucault 2009: 4–5).

Despite the closures, which were celebrated and welcomed, Foucault argues that something of a permanent mark remained in the minds of inhabitants of these cities – the values and images of exclusion, and the social importance they acquired.

Foucault's book begins with the chapter 'Stultifera navis', as he takes the reader on a journey in the 'ship of fools'. The *Narrenschiff* is a literary topos and a painterly theme, but it was also a reality. The exact meaning of sending madmen on the boat is not absolutely clear, but the persons seem to have had an effortless and undemanding existence while floating on a riverboat from city to city. Driven outside the city limits, the madmen were allowed to wander in the open countryside (Foucault 2009: 7). This custom was particularly frequent in Germany along the Rhine. Foucault acknowledges that these ships of fools were possibly pilgrimage boats with their 'highly symbolic cargoes of madmen in search of their reason' (2009: 7).

The position of madmen is nevertheless strategic. They are placed in boats, but also in the transient places at the limits of the city, by the city walls and gates. This exclusion of madmen also 'encloses them' within the walls of the city, which is the threshold and the point of passage. Foucault writes about the fate of the madman:

The position of madmen is nevertheless strategic. They are placed in boats, but also in the transient places at the limits of the city, by the city walls and gates. This exclusion of madmen also 'encloses them' within the walls of the city, which is the threshold and the point of passage.

if he cannot and must not have another *prison* than the *threshold* itself, he is kept at the point of passage. He is put in the interior of the exterior, and inversely. A highly symbolic position, which will doubtless remain his until our own day, if we are willing to admit that what was formerly a visible fortress of order has now become the castle of our conscience (Foucault 2009: 8–9).

This analogy between the 'fortress of order' and the 'castle of consciousness' is a significant spatial and mental parallel, which tells us about the perceived threat and its evolving nature. On the subject of the role of walls and walling in relation to fifteenth-century and later architectural theory and practice, one can consult recent commentaries that go beyond the usual (romanticised) historicism, suggesting a more critical evaluation of this phenomenon (Hirst 2005; Fontana-Giusti 2011).

In a manner that recalls his later discussion of 'heterotopia' (see Chapter 5), Foucault points to a link between water, navigation and madness in the dreams of European men. Foucault thinks that the reason for the figure of the 'ship of fools' becoming the subject of many texts and images lies in the fact that it symbolised a great disquiet dawning on the horizon of European culture at the end of the Middle Ages. 'Madness and madman become major figures, in their ambiguity: menace and mockery, the dizzying unreason of the world, and the feeble ridicule of men' (Foucault 2009: 11).

Foucault thinks that the reason for the figure of the 'ship of fools' becoming the subject of many texts and images lies in the fact that it symbolised a great disquiet dawning on the horizon of European culture at the end of the Middle Ages.

A split appeared first of all between two forms of madness: on the one hand, the madness as in the paintings of Bosch (in the last years of the fifteenth century) and on the other, the madness as described in Erasmus's *In Praise of Folly* (1509). The former sees madness as troubling, obsessive and threatening, 'seemingly revealing the deep secret into which the truth of our world of appearances vanishes', while the latter 'was already madness set at a distance' and caught in the discourse, elaborated in books and preached about at universities. The gap between the two grew from then onward (Foucault 2009: 12–13).

Foucault explains that the sixteenth- and early-seventeenth-century world was still strangely hospitable to madness. Madness was often seen to be at the heart of things – an ironic sign that marks the space between the real and the imaginary. It was understood as some kind of 'mobility of reason' that, according to Foucault, needed no external element (in the form of rational explanation) to reach its true resolution. Being mobile, madness was also like a sudden burst of life – the 'wind of madness', a type of baroque gesture, a *trompe-l'oeil*. Madness appears as such in the tragicomic literary works by Shakespeare, Cervantes and their contemporaries.

Madness was often seen to be at the heart of things – an ironic sign that marks the space between the real and the imaginary. It was understood as some kind of 'mobility of reason' that, according to Foucault, needed no external element (in the form of rational explanation) to reach its true resolution.

By contrast, in the latter half of the seventeenth century, madness found itself isolated and banished during the events that Foucault described as the formation of 'the great confinements', which saw madness condemned, silenced and excluded by the sovereign act of reason. Madness was locked up and put away in a move that had direct economic, political, moral and religious motives and consequences.

The hospital became a place of confinement, allowing the wealthy and the privileged to clean up the increasingly growing and messy city. The poor, the idle, beggars, vagabonds, the debouched, libertines, those with venereal diseases, prostitutes and homosexuals joined the insane behind the walls of places such as the Hôpital Général in Paris.

The perception of the poor, mad, destitute and marginalised changed at this time, as they became perceived as socially dangerous. The late-seventeenth-century elite invented both rational and moral arguments for creating establishments for locking up the poor. The hospital became a place of confinement, allowing the wealthy and the privileged to clean up the increasingly growing and messy city. The poor, the idle, beggars, vagabonds, the debouched, libertines, those with venereal diseases, prostitutes and homosexuals joined the insane behind the walls of places such as the Hôpital Général in Paris.

The Hôpital Général was established at the time when major Royal palaces and other large edifices were built and reinforced; it contained a number of separate units, including Hôpital-Dieu in l'Île de la Cité. In the 1660s, Libéral Bruant (1635–97) was put in charge of the conversion of Louis XIII's old arsenal (the Salpêtrière) into a 'great confinement' that became the Pitié-Salpêtrière Hospital. The time was a dynamic period of Paris's urban development, its architecture and its urban landscape. Significant contributions were made by many: Claude Perrault (1613–88) on the east façade of Louvre (1665–80); Le Vau (1612–70) who, in collaboration with Perrault, worked on the new palace in Versailles; Bruant and Jules Hardouin-Mansart (1646–1708) who worked on Les Invalides (1670–9). The latter became the superintendent of royal buildings, directing the extension of the royal château of Saint-Germain-en-Laye and, from 1675, the château Versailles. In Paris, Hardouin-Mansart's works include the Pont-Royal, the Église Saint-Roch, the Place des Victoires (1684–6) and the Place Vendôme (1690). André Le Notre contributed by landscaping the Tuilleries gardens (1665) that had determined the grand axis of Paris, which still extends westwards to La Défense and beyond.

The emergence of 'confinements' thus coincided with the making of the new city centre, its new landmarks and the solidification of its walls and lineaments as a series of decisive urban gestures. The new buildings and their urban walls determined the spatial configuration of rationalist geometry in service to the monarchy and its prestige. The French monarchy at the time was in the process of establishing itself as the centralised state governed from its restructured capital and from the new palace in Versailles. The overall design of the palaces was geometrically captivating in its aim to delineate the increasing power of the monarch. By compelling the aristocracy to inhabit the new palaces, the king succeeded in putting it under his control, while the grandeur of both the Louvre and Versailles implied the magnificence (and righteousness) of the royal power. There was, therefore, an economy of unfortunate reciprocity between the great confinements for the poor and the centralised royal splendour. The great confinements provided the conditions for the city of Paris and the stately power to develop.

There was, therefore, an economy of unfortunate reciprocity between the great confinements for the poor and the centralised royal splendour. The great confinements provided the conditions for the city of Paris and the stately power to develop.

Foucault stresses that the seventeenth-century confinements had organised punishments rather than medical treatment. The Hôpital Général was not a medical establishment; it was a semi-judicial, administrative institution, which had powers to try, judge and execute outside the courts.

Eventually, during the course of the eighteenth century, from the economic point of view, the value of the internment no longer made sense. Madness would again find itself separated, but this time it was called Unreason (*Déraison*). The divine creative aspect of madness was lost and the mad were isolated (2009: 192). The architecture of the institutions that followed and found itself complicit in the process was conceived as the extension and application of reason.

## 3.2 The Asylum

Italian physician Vincenzo Chiarugi (1759–1820) is today recognized as having liberated psychiatric patients from chains in Santa Dorotea hospital in Florence in 1785–88, therefore several years before Philippe Pinel (1745–1826) did so in France (Gerard 1998: 381–403). According to Foucault, the 1794 event of the unchaining of the mad at the Parisian Bicêtre Hospital by Pinel marked the birth of the asylum. Although the patients were unchained, the doctors who treated the insane did not simply open the asylum to medical knowledge. On the contrary, the asylum is not a free realm of observation, diagnosis and therapeutics but rather

> ... it is a juridical space where one is accused, judged and condemned, and from which one is never released except by the version of this trial in psychological depth, that is, by remorse. Madness will be punished in the asylum, even if it is innocent outside of it (Foucault 2009: 269–72).

Foucault concludes that Pinel and William Tuke (1732–1822) did not introduce a scientific approach, but adopted an authoritarian personality, which borrowed powers from science to justify their actions (2009: 269–72).

Foucault analysed the documents that mention different kinds of madness. He investigated as distinct the perceived attributes of melancholia, hysteria and hypochondria. The symptoms of melancholia were initially (in the sixteenth and early-seventeenth century) linked to the four humours and Foucault discusses early humoural and spiritual explanations of melancholia. These explanations were gradually replaced by the mid- and late- seventeenth-century debate on the origin of melancholia, which emphasised a new approach. In discussing different kinds of madness, Foucault points out that during the classical period, melancholia, hysteria and hypochondria slowly became seen as mental diseases and he identifies a change in the late-eighteenth century when the previous understanding of madness linked to the humours and the dynamics of the body changed into questions of morality and sensibility.

In discussing different kinds of madness, Foucault points out that during the classical period, melancholia, hysteria and hypochondria slowly became seen as mental diseases and he identifies a change in the late-eighteenth century when the previous understanding of madness linked to the humours and the dynamics of the body changed into questions of morality and sensibility.

By writing on doctors and patients, Foucault explored the therapeutics of madness, where the main concern was 'to correct' the individual, to cure his or her nervous fibre and imagination (Foucault 2009: 151). Foucault specifically lists the following instances of cure: *consolidation* of the weak, mobile and irritable fibres; *purification*, consisting of substitution of the blood encumbered with bitter humours with one that is clear; *immersion*, where involvement with water was seen as the purest of all beneficent natural substances; and finally *regulation of movement*, as madness is ultimately irregular agitation of the movement of the spirits, ideas and fibres (2009: 154–65).

Foucault acknowledged that in the classical period, it was futile to try to distinguish physical therapeutics from psychological medications, as psychology simply did not yet exist. According to Foucault, psychology emerged 'not as the truth of madness, but as a sign that madness was now detached from its truth which was unreason'; as such psychology was, according to Foucault, 'adrift', 'insignificant' and aimless in the larger schema of things (2009: 187–8).

According to Foucault, psychology emerged 'not as the truth of madness, but as a sign that madness was now detached from its truth which was unreason'; as such psychology was, according to Foucault, 'adrift', 'insignificant' and aimless in the larger schema of things.

It is in this context that he invokes the importance of Freud's contribution in going back to madness, what Foucault called 'the sovereign violence of a return' (Foucault 2009: 188). Freud took important steps in his 'Five Case Histories'. According to Foucault, Freud went back to madness and reconstituted on the level of language the essential experience of madness that had been reduced to silence by positivism (as in the example of Pierre Janet's *Psychological Healing* (1925) which marks the important often debated difference between the two thinkers). In doing so, Foucault continued, Freud crucially restored the possibility of a dialogue with unreason, whose experience had been masked by psychology (Foucault 2009: 188).

According to Foucault, Freud went back to madness and reconstituted on the level of language the essential experience of madness that had been reduced to silence by positivism. In doing so, Foucault continued, Freud crucially restored the possibility of a dialogue with unreason, whose experience had been masked by psychology.

*Madness and Civilisation* had a tremendous impact upon a public that was in a state of ignorance about psychiatry and the roots of its knowledge. A sociologist and a colleague of Foucault, Robert Castel summarised the 1960s reactions to *Madness and Civilisation* by pointing out how this book worked on various levels: it was possible to read it simultaneously as an academic thesis (a continuation of the work of Bachelard and Canguilhem) and as an evocation of the dark powers of the forbidden, in the manner of Lautréamont or Antonin Artaud. Castel writes:

> it was this paradoxical montage that provided the unique status of this work. To some it was fascinating, to others irritating, or both at once. But believing in the theses of the work did not imply any precise political option, or any project for practical change (Castel 1986: 42–4).

The book was significant for the unity of Foucault's work, attaching it firmly to the notion of 'power' and to the future dual concept 'power-knowledge'. As Foucault himself reflected: 'All of that emerged like something written in invisible ink that began to appear on the paper when the right reagent was added, which was the word *power*' (Trombadori 1999: 77–8).

### Architecture and madness

Bernard Tschumi's references to Foucault's discourse on madness appeared in the essay entitled 'Madness and Combinative' (Tschumi 1996: 174–90) and in the design of Les Follies of Parc de la Villette, Paris. In this essay, Tschumi argues that madness is a constant point of reference throughout the urban Park of La Villette as it 'illustrates a characteristic situation at the end of the twentieth century – that of disjunction and dissociation between the use, form and social value' (Tschumi 1996: 175). He argues that non-coincidences between being and meaning, man and object have been explored from Nietzsche to Foucault, from Joyce to Lacan, adding that people and objects are not part of the homogeneous and coherent world:

It is not necessary to recall in this context how Michel Foucault, in *Madness and Civilisation*, analyses the manner in which insanity raises questions of a sociological, philosophical and psychoanalytic nature. On one hand, that normality ('good' architecture; typologies, modern movement dogmas, rationalism, and other 'isms' of recent history) is only one possibility among those offered by the combination of 'genetics' of architectural elements. On the other, that, just as all collectivities require lunatics, deviants, and criminals to mark their own negativity, so architecture needs extremes and interdictions to inscribe the reality of its constant oscillation between the pragmatics of the built realm and the absoluteness of concepts. There is no intention here to descend into an intellectual fascination with madness, but rather to stress that madness articulates something that is often negated in order to preserve a fragile cultural or social order (1996: 175).

Tschumi argues that madness is a constant point of reference throughout the urban Park of La Villette as it 'illustrates a characteristic situation at the end of the twentieth century – that of disjunction and dissociation between the use, form and social value'.

There is no intention here to descend into an intellectual fascination with madness, but rather to stress that madness articulates something that is often negated in order to preserve a fragile cultural or social order.

Although little has been argued about the relevance of Foucault's work for Tschumi, its effects on the Swiss architect is profoundly evident. In this writing,

Tschumi challenges norms of typologies, the so-called 'good architecture' and various dogmas such as those of the modern movement and rationalism seeing them as possibilities that emerged due to the conditions of architecture. Like Foucault, he sees them only as possibilities that became reality within the settings established by the society and its norms, where misfits, the poorly adjusted and deviants also have a role.

Even more traditionally minded architectural historians have reacted to the themes of madness and the ground opened up by Foucault's texts. In his two-part article in the *AA Files* entitled 'Sickness, Madness and Crime as the Grounds of Form', Robin Middleton explored the late-eighteenth- and nineteenth-century architecture of hospitals, asylums and prisons. He looked at the dynamics of their rise at the end of the eighteenth century and their climax in the mid-nineteenth century. Middleton gave his summary of Foucault's discourse as he analysed the relevant architectural examples. He wrote:

> **Whatever the spring, the poor were encouraged henceforth to work, the sick and the insane were to be cured to the same end, and criminals, likewise, redeemed. The instrument of reform, surprisingly enough, was to be architecture (Middleton 1992: 17).**

Middleton states the widespread eighteenth-century beliefs about the power of the architectural form by acknowledging the rationalists' position: that buildings designed with precision and reasonableness could affect behavioural, health and ethical issues almost unaided. He states that between 1772 and 1778 there were more than 200 proposals made for the re-establishment of the Hôtel-Dieu in Paris; out of this, more than fifty were architectural proposals. He describes many of them, from those by C. N. Ledoux and J. F. T. Chalgrin, via Pierre Panseron, J. B. Leroy and C. F. Viel, to Dr Antoine Petit's project at Belleville and various projects at Île des Cygnes (including the grand pavilion-type model for a series of hospitals designed by a committee of the Académie des Sciences in 1788). Many of these were subsequently published in the seminal work of the architect and professor of architecture at the École Polytechnique, Jean-Nicholas-Louis Durand (1760–1834): *Receuil et parallèle des édifice de tout genre, ancient and modern,* 1799–1800 (Middleton 1992: 16–30). Middleton's examples thus support Foucault's arguments in a telling way.

Middleton states the widespread eighteenth-century beliefs about the power of the architectural form by acknowledging the rationalists' position: that buildings designed with precision and reasonableness could affect behavioural, health and ethical issues almost unaided.

### 3.3 The Clinic

*The Birth of the Clinic* (1963) is Foucault's archaeology of medical perception and a critique of modern clinical medicine. It continues the line of critique introduced by *Madness and Civilisation* that would be followed in *Discipline and Punishment* and *The History of Sexuality*. The book is concerned with the emergence of medical science, focusing on the period from the French Revolution in 1789 to the arrival of medical treatises such as the one by François-Joseph-Victor Broussais in the 1820s. Foucault is not simply concerned with medical history in the traditional sense; rather, he investigates a number of problems that cut across medical science. His interest is in the conditions that had brought medical science to the fore and how these conditions related to the general state of knowledge at the time. He is attentive to the limits of this knowledge and its implications for other discourses and practices.

Foucault is not simply concerned with medical history in the traditional sense; rather, he investigates a number of problems that cut across medical science. His interest is in the conditions that had brought medical science to the fore

and how these conditions related to the general state of

knowledge at the time.

He himself considered *The Birth of the Clinic* to be a book about space, language and death, about the act of seeing – the gaze and the practice of observation. The main argument follows the way in which clinical medicine came to exist as a discipline established upon observation, where the gaze of the doctor came to determine 'the domain of medicine's experience and the structure of its rationality' (Foucault 2010: xvii). For Foucault, the nature of the observation and analysis of a single diseased organ depended entirely upon the established organisational practices at that time and any examination, diagnosis and treatment followed the same epistemological pattern.

Foucault describes the series of events on two levels: first, specific events linked to the late-eighteenth- and early-nineteenth-century birth of modern anatomo-clinical medicine based on the medical gaze and the dissection of corpses; and second, in the political sphere, the general shift that promoted the increased commitment to the health of the population overall. *The Birth of the Clinic* therefore makes a distinction between the 'medicine of species' and the 'medicine of social spaces', referring to separate modalities of medical practice. The former was related to classifying diseases, diagnosing and treating patients mainly in the family, and in a relationship agreed between a doctor and patient. The latter was concerned with public health; its actions included preventing outbreaks of epidemic diseases and general measures of hygiene.

*The Birth of the Clinic* therefore makes a distinction between

the 'medicine of species' and the 'medicine of social spaces',

referring to separate modalities of medical practice. The former was related to classifying diseases, diagnosing and treating patients mainly in the family, and in a relationship agreed between a doctor and patient. The latter was concerned with public health; its actions included preventing outbreaks of epidemic diseases and general measures of hygiene.

### *The birth of the scientific gaze, the operating table and the centrality of death*

In respect of the former, Foucault contrasts two approaches that show the important change in attitude in diagnosing diseases and in the treatment of patients, which, according to him, reflects the change in the underlying conditions of medical knowledge that emerged in the beginning of the nineteenth century. His two examples include first, Pierre Pomme (a well-known French physician), who in the 1750s treated and apparently 'cured' a hysteric by making her take ten or twelve hours of baths per day for ten months, and second, Antoine Laurent Bayle, who in the 1820s, less than 100 years later, took an entirely different approach to treating a patient, as he observed the link between the lesion on the brain of a patient and general paralysis. This observation that occurred in the practice of pathological anatomy has helped Bayle to establish an important link that helped him to accurately diagnose paresis (general paralysis) in a comprehensive and clear manner.

These two profoundly different approaches, according to Foucault, have determined the change that brought medical science to the fore. The difference is tiny but important, he argues. Bayle's qualitative description based on observation is like a picture that guides our gaze into the world of visibility, while Pomme's is a fantasy without much observation. Foucault states that the change is not due to any spontaneous break with the imaginary approaches. What is at stake is a new perspective, an approach that looks at the symptoms and their connections inside the body.

## What is at stake is a new perspective, an approach that looks at the symptoms and their connections inside the body.

In acknowledging and defining this moment in the history of medicine, Foucault made an important space-related observation: he argued that the gaze of the doctor strengthened the belief in the link between knowledge and pain, as if the signs of pain had been redistributed in space in which bodies of patients and eyes of the clinician met.

Thus, Foucault argues, the medical gaze (and its spatial setup) became increasingly identified as a dominant factor not only in medicine, but in the underlying episteme of the time. Its nature is complex: the gaze is reserved and its strength comes from this restraint. In Foucault's words, it is not enough for it to exercise prudence or scepticism: the gaze has to restore the truth in accordance with the 'genesis of the events of the body'. In this sense, the gaze is also 'analytic': it has to have its logic, which depends entirely on the quality of its perception (Foucault 2010: 133).

## Thus, Foucault argues, the medical gaze (and its spatial setup) became increasingly identified as a dominant factor not only in medicine, but in the underlying episteme of the time.

The procedures that supported this perception and guaranteed its scientific accuracy involved the cutting of corpses. The observations based on open bodies were analysed and the knowledge acquired in this way gradually came to form the science of pathological anatomy that took centre stage within medical sciences. Crucially, according to Foucault, this had consequences upon other sciences and on the conditions of knowledge in general. The structure of scientific thinking, which worked through dissection and observation while penetrating into the interiority of things, gradually became an assumed overall approach in scientific investigation.

# The structure of scientific thinking, which worked through dissection and observation while penetrating into the interiority of things, gradually became an assumed overall approach in scientific investigation.

In these practices and processes, Foucault acknowledges the role of the 'operating table' as

> a *tabula*, that enables thought to operate upon the entities of our world, to put them in order, to divide them into classes, to group them according to names that designate their similarities and their differences – the table upon which, since the beginning of time the language has intersected space (Foucault 1991: xvii).

The condition of this table-related space of observation and juxtaposition is the legacy of clinical medicine to the sciences overall. The development of clinical medicine had a number of consequences for the architecture of the nineteenth century and later. These are evident on at least two levels: directly, in designing new hospitals with larger, brighter spaces for clinical practice; and indirectly, in the practice of inspection, dissection and revitalisation of old buildings as in the architectural practice of Viollet-le-Duc (1814–79) who was commissioned to restore the Romanesque abbey of Vézelay and who was the advocate of the keen attitude for the restoration of old buildings that developed in France in the 1830s. This attitude for inspecting, cutting and restoring (curing) the buildings relates to the dominant model of thinking at the time, which, according to Foucault, was based on the medical gaze initially deployed in pathological anatomy and clinical practice.

The condition of this table-related space of observation and juxtaposition is the legacy of clinical medicine to the sciences overall.

What becomes prominent in Foucault's analysis is the critique of how, in the knowledge structure of clinical medicine, death gained the absolute position. The dead body becomes the levelling 'ground zero' from where the scientific process of tracing back and mapping down the events begins. Foucault acknowledges the strangeness of this centrality of death in Western clinical medicine and in subsequent scientific knowledge. He writes,

> It will no doubt remain a decisive fact about our culture that its first scientific discourse concerning the individual had to pass *through this stage of death*. Western man could constitute himself in his own eyes as an object of science, he grasped himself within his language and gave himself in himself and by himself, and a discursive existence only in the opening created by his own elimination (Foucault 2010: 243).

What becomes prominent in Foucault's analysis is the critique of how, in the knowledge structure of clinical medicine, death gained the absolute position. The dead body becomes the levelling 'ground zero' from where the scientific process of tracing back and mapping down the events begins.

Foucault links the strangeness of the nineteenth-century centrality of death to the absence of the gods. He argues that the experience of individuality in modern culture is bound up with that of death:

from Hölderlin's Empedocles to Nietzsche's Zarathustra, and on to
Freudian man, an obstinate relation to death prescribes to the universal
its singular face and lends to each individual the power of being heard
forever... (Foucault 2010: 243).

Throughout the nineteenth century, death-related concerns emerged in social
practices and norms concerned with fighting the spread of deadly diseases through
the development of hygiene. This was particularly the case in big cities, which
faced mass loss of life in the areas of high density where the urban poor lived.
This condition introduced the planning of new type of cemeteries on the edges of
the city. Prominent examples include Père Lachaise (1804) in Paris, Kensal Green
(1832), Highgate (1839) and another five from the 'magnificent seven' in Victorian
London. In Foucault's critical analysis, the space of cemeteries belongs to the other
spaces (heterotopia) discussed later in this book (Chapter 5: Spatiality / Aesthetics).

### Architecture, clinic and the city

Foucault contributed to the volume *Les machine a guérir* (Machines for Cure), the
book on the origins of the modern hospital co-written with architects Blandine
Barret-Kriegel, Anne Thalamy and Bruno Fortier (1995). The initial work for
*Les machines a guérir* was the product of two research projects: *Genealogy of
Collective Equipment*, headed by Foucault, and *Politics of space in Paris at the end
of the Ancien Régime*, originally led by Bruno Fortier in 1976. The themes that
were raised in this research include the development of hospitalisation, with an
emphasis on the spatial organisation of its buildings as well as the mechanisms
by which public health was carried out. The volume is an intersection and a
contribution to both architectural history and the history of medicine.

In the section entitled 'The political geography of health',

Vidler makes reference to Foucault's analyses of the

consequences of the development of medicine upon studies of

urban pathology and subsequent policies on urban hygiene.

We find further impact of Foucault's studies on medical history in Anthony Vidler's account of the reorganisation of the hospitals at the end of the eighteenth and the beginning of the nineteenth century (Vidler 1989: 51–73). In the section entitled 'The political geography of health', Vidler makes reference to Foucault's analyses of the consequences of the development of medicine upon studies of urban pathology and subsequent policies on urban hygiene. He writes that during the revolutionary period, the vision of the natural distribution of wealth coincided, as Michel Foucault has noted, with the utopia of 'natural' medicine. Vidler quotes Foucault's explanation about the nineteenth-century ideal of returning to the natural origins of medicine through prevention of diseases by means of dietary instructions and universal exercise, which would make doctors and hospitals obsolete. Moreover, Vidler argues that the entire discipline of urban pathology developed after 1789, beginning with the *Essai sur la topographie-physique et médicale de Paris* by the doctor Audin-Rouvière, and ending with the urban 'surgery' of Haussmann (Vidler 1989: 71). Vidler concludes that this is not an unusual example as the promise of prevention of diseases affected the designs of many urban utopias from Ledoux's Ideal City of Chaux, to Le Corbusier's Ville Verte (Vidler 1989: 71).

Moreover, Vidler argues that the entire discipline of urban pathology developed after 1789, beginning with the *Essai sur la topographie-physique et médicale de Paris* by the doctor Audin-Rouvière, and ending with the urban 'surgery' of Haussmann.

In his later writing 'The Scenes of the Street: Transformations in Ideal and Reality: 1750–1871', Vidler borrows from Foucault's eighteenth-century sources, such as Desault's description of clinical surgery in the Hôtel-Dieu of 1781 quoted in *The Birth of the Clinic* (Vidler 2011: 16–130). Again, he follows Foucault's main thesis about the transformation of the scientific episteme at the end of the eighteenth century in respect to clinical medicine and he maps the potential corresponding phenomena in architecture and urbanism. In that respect, Vidler recognises how Pierre Patte, the student of Jacques-Francois Blondel and the author of the 1765 Plan of Paris 'brought together in a single plan the various projects for town squares (*grandes places*) that had been submitted in the competition for the placement of Louis XV's statue' (Vidler 2011: 30–1). Patte did this by means of careful juxtaposition of various parts that were put together in the new plan in an almost surgical manner, Vidler writes. Although Patte's plan came only twelve years after Laugier's treatise, Vidler recognises an important difference in the approach:

> **Laugier's architect was a gardener, Patte's was a surgeon. The city as a forest, to be tamed by the arts of cultivation, was now seen as a body in various states of sickness and disease, to be cured by the arts of medicine (Vidler 2011: 32).**

Vidler extends the Foucauldian medical analogy further by stating that the city that was first seen as a sick patient was soon to be considered to be a healing doctor capable of its own therapy. Vidler states that on the eve of the revolution, scientists and doctors turned their attention to the city as a whole, 'not just to cleanse its parts but to develop its innate therapeutic character' (Vidler 2011: 34). He lists ventilation, lighting, drainage, new hospitals and the replacement of old cemeteries with new as instances of curing the social disease, which was seen as a political and a civic problem. Using Foucault's sources to explain the urbanism of the last years of the ancient regime, Vidler stated the widespread opinion among the people who were involved in running Paris:

> **The institution of the right ordered state, with its population trained from birth in habits of cleanliness, healthy exercise, and celebration of their freedom from social ills, would finally render medicine unnecessary. The city would then take on its rightful role as the site of health and its sustenance, and the street, the public room par excellence, would retrieve the civic and festive functions ... (Vidler 2011: 35).**

This vision of the city as healthy, liberating and festive was subsequently exercised at the time of revolution, and as such this vision has remained an ideal in the domain of planning.

## 3.4 The Prison

Foucault's interpreters agree that the philosopher's remarks on the difference between archaeology and genealogy are somewhat vague.

In contrast to the previous 'archaeological' approach, *Discipline and Punish* (1991a) (*Surveiller et punir*: 1975) marks Foucault's return to social critique and the transition to his 'genealogical' approach to history. Foucault's interpreters agree that the philosopher's remarks on the difference between archaeology and genealogy are somewhat vague. Indeed, the tools Foucault uses to practice both methods appear to be the same; however, if archaeology addresses a level where concepts and discourses are organised to produce workable forms of knowledge, genealogy deals with the same level of knowledge and culture now described at a level where the grounds of the true and the false come to be distinguished and analysed via mechanisms of power (O'Farrell 2007).

However, if archaeology addresses a level where concepts and discourses are organised to produce workable forms of knowledge, genealogy deals with the same level of knowledge and culture now described at a level where the grounds of the true and the false come to be distinguished and analysed via mechanisms of power.

As seen in *Madness and Civilisation, The Birth of the Clinic* and *The Order of Things*, archaeologies allowed Foucault to operate at a level that displaced the primacy of the author as a speaking and knowing subject that was traditionally found in phenomenology. Archaeology's domain and scope were restricted to comparisons of discourses belonging to different periods and could not address the causes of the transition from one way of thinking to another. With genealogy, Foucault intended to resolve this deficiency and demonstrate that a given system of thought was the result of the conditions of history, not the outcome of rationally inevitable trends. Foucault's genealogy is not a linear search for origins. He describes it as investigation into recording the 'singularity of events' about things which 'we tend to feel [are] without history' (Foucault 1977: 139).

With genealogy, Foucault intended to resolve this deficiency and demonstrate that a given system of thought was the result of the conditions of history, not the outcome of rationally inevitable trends. Foucault's genealogy is not a linear search for origins. He describes it as investigation into recording the 'singularity of events' about things which 'we tend to feel [are] without history'.

Echoing Nietzsche's *Genealogy of Morals*, Foucault aimed to demonstrate the plural and often contradictory past that reveals traces of the effects that power relations have had upon truth. By questioning and analysing presumed truths in *Discipline and Punish*, Foucault argues that truth is often discovered by chance and backed by the workings of power in the pursuit of its own interests.

While investigating the emergence of a new kind of imprisonment, *Discipline and Punish* examines the disappearance of the old system of punishment that was carried on in public executions. The incarceration that replaced torture and killing was accompanied by the resurgence of the gaze, real or imaginary. Foucault explains how such change in punitive practice became a means of more effective control and how this new mode of punishment became the model for control of an entire society and its various institutions and practices. The deployment of this model, which became known as panopticism (see below), was not a result of the decisions made by some central controlling body or institution, or by conspiracy. On the contrary, Foucault demonstrated how techniques and institutions developed for different purposes joined up and gradually applied the principles of panopticism in order to create the modern system of disciplinary power.

Foucault explains how such change in punitive practice became a means of more effective control and how this new mode of punishment became the model for control of an entire society and its various institutions and practices.

Foucault's description of modern 'disciplinary' society outlines three primary techniques of control: hierarchical observation, normalising judgment and the examination – practised generally at various instances. Control over people can be achieved to a great extent simply by observation. There is thus a need for a series of hierarchically ordered and strategically placed observers through whom observed information passes from lower to higher levels. A perfect system of observation that was sought after would allow one guard to see everything, as in Jeremy Bentham's *Panopticon* (see below).

Foucault links Bentham's design to Le Vau's menagerie at Versailles (c. 1663), the first-ever menagerie, where different animals were not, as they were traditionally, distributed in a park (Loisel 1912: 104–7). Rather, a centre with an octagonal pavilion consisted of a room raised on a first floor, where the king had large windows on each side to look at the cages with animals. Late

Baroque architecture and landscape design of this kind, Foucault argued, provided a useful series of precedents to the eighteenth-century designs of hospitals, asylums and prisons.

Late Baroque architecture and landscape design of this kind,

Foucault argued, provided a useful series of precedents to the

eighteenth-century designs of hospitals, asylums and prisons.

### *Bodies, space and* dispositifs

Foucault analysed and defined the mechanisms of discipline, which he called *dispositifs* – by which he meant a heterogeneous apparatus consisting of discourses, institutions, architectural forms, regulatory decisions, laws, administrative measures, scientific statements, and philosophical, moral and philanthropic propositions, all of which were involved in maintaining the exercise of power within a society (Foucault 1986: 194–228). As these disciplinary mechanisms are spatial in nature, involving a symbiosis of architecture and another doctrine, we shall briefly outline a selection of Foucault's examples.

Foucault looked at the following *dispositifs*: 1) the art of distribution, 2) the control of activity, 3) the organisational genesis, and 4) the composition of forces (Foucault 1991a: 135–70). Particularly relevant for architecture is the art of distribution. This includes the placement of bodies in space and, according to Foucault, has been made achievable by means of several techniques.

Foucault identifies the techniques as the following: 1) the deployment of *enclosures* – the diverse spaces of 'disciplinary monotony' such as boarding schools, military barracks, manufacturing spaces (i.e. workshops and factories) that were compared with the monasteries, fortresses and walled towns; 2) the *partitioning*, where the enclosure is divided so that each individual has a

From the Discussion between Foucault and Bernard-Henri Lévy (1981).

place (and each place its individual) and where distribution in groups should be avoided; 3) the *functional organisation* of buildings and sites with codes of usage such as hospitals, prisons and factories; 4) the *ranking* (as discipline is the art of rank) – a technique of transformation and circulation of disciplinary units and arrangements; and 5) the *composition of forces* which is about the art of tactics.

Foucault acknowledges how various systems of discipline such as 'cells', 'places' and 'ranks' create complex spaces that are at once architectural, functional and hierarchical. He writes about them,

> It is spaces that provide fixed positions and permit circulation; they carve
> out individual segments and establish operational links; they mark places
> and indicate values; they guarantee the obedience of the individuals, but
> also a better economy of time and gesture (Foucault 1991a: 148).

Foucault states that these spaces of mixed character are at the same time *real*, because they govern the disposition of such objects as buildings, rooms and furniture, but also *ideal*, as they project the ideal arrangement of assessments and hierarchies. He refers to *'tableaux vivants'* (living pictures) as the first operation of discipline and cellular power that had the task of transforming the 'confused, useless or dangerous multitudes' into 'ordered multiplicities'. Here the twin operations of distribution and analysis on the one hand and supervision and intelligibility on the other are bound up in this eighteenth-century organisational chart, which was both a technique of power and a procedure of knowledge (Foucault 1991a: 148).

He refers to *'tableaux vivants'* (living pictures) as the first

operation of discipline and cellular power that had the task of

transforming the 'confused, useless or dangerous multitudes'

into 'ordered multiplicities'.

### Timetable and correlation of bodies

Foucault analysed the instances of control such as the timetable, which he identified as the model based on monastic life containing the establishment of three methods: rhythm, occupation and cycles of repetition – all remarkably spatial. This is followed by 'temporal elaboration of the act', described as an anatomo-chronological schema of behaviour primarily developed by the military and later applied in the schools such as École Polytechnique.

The temporal elaboration of the act (i.e. behaviour linked to specific times), continued Foucault, led to *the correlation of the body and gesture* that imposes the 'best gesture' and the overall position of the body in order to make it more efficient; for example, teaching pupils how to sit when reading and writing. This was followed by *the body-object articulation*, understood along the same line of rationality and efficiency. The final principle of *exhaustive use* is based on the premise of non-idleness, where idleness is understood as both moral offence and economic dishonesty. Therefore, the timetable needs to be filled in.

Foucault analyses the example of the 1667 Parisian Gobelins school for children chosen to be educated and instructed in tapestry makings. New techniques for taking charge of the time of individual existence had been developed, regulating relations of bodies and forces, for the purpose of an accumulation of time dedicated to work and for turning this work into profit. Foucault explains how the disciplinary time was imposed on pedagogical practice – specifying training that involved exercises of increasing difficulty, which reveals a linear, evaluative process whose moments are orientated towards a terminal point such as the end of education and training (Foucault 1991a: 157–9).

New techniques for taking charge of the time of individual existence had been developed, regulating relations of bodies and forces, for the purpose of an accumulation of time dedicated to work and for turning this work into profit.

The final instance of discipline outlined by Foucault – the *composition of forces* – is about the arrangement of tactics, the art of constructing (with bodies, activities and trained aptitudes) mechanisms in which the impact is increased by their calculated combination. Foucault writes that in the eighteenth century, tactics was considered the highest form of disciplinary practice and as such, this knowledge became the foundation of all military practice (Foucault 1991a: 167). He writes,

> It may be that war as strategy is a continuation of politics. But it must not be forgotten that 'politics' has been conceived as a continuation, if not exactly and directly of war, at least of the military model as a fundamental means of preventing civil disorder (Foucault 1991a: 168).

This leads Foucault to conclude that while eighteenth-century jurists and philosophers were seeking a primal model for the construction of the social body, it was the military men (the technicians of discipline) who set the procedures for the individual and collective coercion of bodies.

This leads Foucault to conclude that while eighteenth-century jurists and philosophers were seeking a primal model for the construction of the social body, it was the military men (the technicians of discipline) who set the procedures for the individual and collective coercion of bodies.

### Invisibility of power

One of the main features of the disciplinary power is that it is exercised through invisibility. Prior to the eighteenth century, argues Foucault, power was seen and displayed through the visibility of the sovereign power of kings and the 'spectacle of the scaffold of execution' (Foucault 1991a: 32–69). Individuals upon whom it was exercised were able to remain in the background and even hide, unless directly approached. This model was now reversed: new disciplinary power imposes compulsory visibility upon those whom it subjects to discipline, while those in power remain invisible.

This model was now reversed: new disciplinary power imposes compulsory visibility upon those whom it subjects to discipline, while those in power remain invisible.

Further control is imposed by the practice of examination that situates individuals in a 'field of documentation and statistics' (Foucault 1991a: 189). Voluntarily or not, these individuals allow power systems to control them by means of attendance records, exams or patients' charts in hospitals. On the basis of these statistics, those in control can establish norms that in turn become a basis for knowledge.

Another feature of power is its preoccupation with what people have not done, i.e. a person's not doing what is required. This concern illustrates the main function of modern disciplinary systems: to correct non-standard behaviour, where the aim is not punishment but reform. Reform means coming to live by society's standards and norms. Discipline through imposing precise norms ('normalisation') is different from the older system of judicial punishment, which judges each action as allowed or not by the law. The idea of normalisation became pervasive in modern society as standards were forged for educational programmes, medical practice and industrial processes.

In all these instances of Foucault's analysis, which include invisibility of power, examination and normalisation, the relationship between power and knowledge is far closer than in the traditional model understood as 'knowledge is power'. Foucault's point is that the goals of power and the goals of knowledge cannot be separated for the study of human beings: in knowing we control and in controlling we know.

## Foucault's point is that the goals of power and the goals of knowledge cannot be separated for the study of human beings: in knowing we control and in controlling we know.

### *Panopticism, diagram and the gaze*

Jeremy Bentham's *Panopticon* (1791) was, for Foucault, an ideal architectural model of modern disciplinary power. It was conceived as a design for a prison and planned for each inmate being separated in a cell, unseen to all the others. At the same time, each prisoner was always visible to a prison officer situated in a central tower. The officer would not always see each inmate; the point is that he could do so at any time if he so wished. As prisoners would never know whether they were being observed, they would need to behave as if they were. As a result, control would be achieved by internal monitoring – i.e. the gaze would become internalised and discipline would be exercised by means

of the imaginary gaze of the prison guard. This is the principle of panopticism.
It spreads beyond prisons to any system of control and disciplinary power
such as factories, hospitals and schools. Although Bentham was never able to
build a Panopticon, the principle of panopticism has come to permeate almost
every aspect of contemporary society, as it became the instrument through
which modern discipline replaced the pre-modern sovereignty of kings and
judges. Foucault understood the panopticon as the diagram of modern power.
He stated that the Panopticon must not be understood as a building: it is a
mechanism of power (*dispositif*) reduced to its essential form – a diagram of
political technology.

Foucault explained that he came across the concept of Panopticon when
he studied the origins of clinical medicine and the hospital architecture of
the second half of the eighteenth century, when the reform of medical
practice was underway. He wanted to know how the medical gaze was
institutionalised, how it became inscribed into social space and how the new
form of the hospital was at once the effect and the support of a new type of
gaze. Foucault's examination of various architectural projects for hospitals led
him to notice that the whole problem of visibility of bodies, individuals and
things, under a system of centralised observation, became the main principle
(Foucault 1986: 146). Foucault brings in the example of the École Militaire in
Paris, which had the future soldiers housed in a building with a centralised
plan, behind cells with glass walls, so that they were constantly under the gaze
of their superiors. Bentham's brother had apparently witnessed this structure
and communicated it back to his reform-inclined sibling, who gave it the
name 'panopticon' – thus crowning the concept with its meaning of all-seeing
(Foucault 1991a: 316).

Foucault explained that he came across the concept of
Panopticon when he studied the origins of clinical medicine
and the hospital architecture of the second half of the

eighteenth century, when the reform of medical practice was underway. He wanted to know how the medical gaze was institutionalised, how it became inscribed into social space and how the new form of the hospital was at once the effect and the support of a new type of gaze.

Foucault elaborated on the gaze and the diagram of panopticism to illustrate a particular dynamic of power relations and disciplinary mechanisms. To some extent, Foucault's ideas about the imaginary gaze of the prison or hospital guard have their background in Lacan's concept of the psychoanalytic gaze, which refers to the state of unease and anxiety provoked by the feeling that one might be under observation. The effect of this feeling is the internalised gaze being linked to the loss of freedom and autonomy of the subject, which in turn provokes fear (Lacan 1987: 67–78). Based on surveillance, modern relations of social control are therefore 'the exact reverse of the spectacle', argued Foucault.

To some extent, Foucault's ideas about the imaginary gaze of the prison or hospital guard have their background in Lacan's concept of the psychoanalytic gaze, which refers to the state of unease and anxiety provoked by the feeling that one might be under observation. The effect of this feeling is the internalised gaze being linked to the loss of freedom and autonomy of the subject, which in turn provokes fear.

In regards to the spectacle in monarchical systems, Foucault states that the disappearance of public killings marked the decline of the public spectacle. He argues that in addition to this change, the modern rituals of execution introduced another modification: the elimination of pain. This was due to the fact that the punishment gradually became the most hidden part of the penal process, as the tendency was to conceal its violent (hence primitive) nature from a society ruled by reason.

The punishment thus becomes more abstract, and its effectiveness results from its inevitability, not from the intensity of its fatal experience (Foucault 1991a: 19). The power of spectacle declined and disappeared with the replacement of emperors and kings by 'disciplines' and 'machines'. While it might be argued that imprisonments, forced labour and penal servitude are still physical penalties, the relationship between the punishment and the body is now structurally different. Foucault states that the prisoners are no longer in the amphitheatre or on the stage, but in the panoptic machine, created by the effects of power.

## The power of spectacle declined and disappeared with the replacement of emperors and kings by 'disciplines' and 'machines'.

In concluding his thoughts on pantopticism, Foucault argues that the formation of the disciplinary society is connected with a number of broad historical processes – economic, juridico-political and scientific – of which it forms a part. He underlines that generally, disciplines are techniques for assuring the ordering of human complexities, something that has always been linked to any system of power. More specific to the eighteenth century, these disciplinary mechanisms, according to Foucault, represent an increase in both the docility and the utility of the system, in part driven by the conditions of the demographic increase of the population and by the increase of production.

Regarding docility, Foucault argues that this panoptic modality of power at an elementary physical level does not depend on the formal political structures of a society. The prison, he argues, with all the corrective technology at its disposal, has been resituated at the point where the legal power to punish has turned into a disciplinary power to observe. In that sense, Foucault makes an important point that the control is due not to the 'universal consciousness of the law that generalized the power to punish', but rather to its 'regular extension, the indefinitely minute web of panoptic techniques' (Foucault 1991a: 224).

In that sense, Foucault makes an important point that the control is due not to the 'universal consciousness of the law that generalized the power to punish', but rather to its 'regular extension, the indefinitely minute web of panoptic techniques'.

In respect to utility, panoptical disciplinary power could also be seen as a technique where the body is reduced as a political force at a minimum cost to generate maximum usefulness. This condition has been incorporated by the capitalist economy and gave rise to the system whose techniques of submitting bodies became dominant. Foucault called this instance 'political anatomy' and as such it applied within diverse regimes, apparatuses and institutions (Foucault 1991a: 221).

While these techniques have a history behind them, what emerges as new in the eighteenth century is that they become combined and generalised, reaching a level at which the formation of knowledge and the increase of power regularly reinforce one another in a circular process. Foucault saw this point as an instance where disciplines crossed the 'technological' threshold (i.e. spread themselves across various fields). His examples included first the hospital, then the school and later the workshop. He states that these institutions became apparatuses themselves, where the growth of power could lead to an increase of knowledge. It was this link within the systems that, Foucault argues, gave rise to clinical medicine, psychiatry, child psychology, the system of education and the rationalisation of labour. Foucault emphasises,

> **It is this double process, then: an epistemological 'thaw' through a refinement of power relations; a multiplication of the effects of power through the formation and accumulation of new forms of knowledge. (Foucault 1991a: 224).**

Architecture's complicity in these processes has been paramount. Since the emergence of Foucault's discussions on panopticism, it has become impossible to see architecture as neutral, simply aesthetic or merely functional. Out of all Foucault's work, this revelation seminally elaborated in *Discipline and Punish* has attracted architects' attention the most.

Architecture's complicity in these processes has been paramount. Since the emergence of Foucault's discussions on panopticism, it has become impossible to see architecture as neutral, simply aesthetic or merely functional.

### *Architecture and spaces of discipline*

It is important to analyse how Foucault's understanding of discipline is relevant on many levels of architecture, as architects consider spatial relations, structures, gaze, visibility, sight lines and views whenever they design. In that sense, the practice of critical analysis has been theoretically strengthened by Foucault's ideas, as architects and scholars have studied and endorsed the contribution of Foucault's texts on hospitals, asylums and prisons.

Anthony Vidler's book *The Writing of the Walls: Architectural Theory in the Late Enlightenment* (1989) opened up a new space of discourse for architects who aimed not only to reconsider the architecture of the eighteenth century but also to question many of architecture's disciplinary premises. The history of this period – often labelled as 'neo-classicism' or 'architecture in the Age of Reason' – was here readdressed in the light of concerns for the structure of knowledge, for the emergence of institutions and for the distribution of power. Vidler makes direct and implied references to Foucault, which gives this book a distinct theoretical dimension. The chapter entitled 'Design of Punishment, Concepts of the Prison before the Revolution' takes the arguments from *Discipline and Punish* as its theoretical premise and departs into archival research and clarification of the concepts and backgrounds.

Elsewhere, Vidler is critical of Foucault's interpreters as he confronts the generally assumed identity of the terms 'spatial' and 'monumental'. Vidler acknowledges the potential for misperception and clarifies Foucault's distinction (Vidler 1992: 172). He asks for caution and the distinction to be observed, as the 'spatial' is a dimension that opposes the 'monumental'. The term spatial is larger in scope and can be used to contextualise the specific monument into a general map of forces in the context of the city. Vidler points out that this was recognised by Situationists and by Henri Lefebvre.

Vidler critically reviewed OMA's scheme for the renovation of a 'panoptical' prison at Arnhem (1979–80) where, according to him, the critical intervention is on the pictorial level: the scheme proposed 'cutting through the tower' as cutting through the centre of the disciplinary apparatus. Vidler states that this would seem to be no more than the liberal 'cancelling' of the old, panoptical functions of the prison, echoing the architect's reading of Foucault (1992: 194–5). Although Foucault's discourse on power and discipline has significantly informed the strategies of the Office for Metropolitan Architecture (OMA) and other practices of similar generations, it is important to avoid vulgarisation of Foucault's concepts, Vidler argued (1992: 195).

He points out that Foucault always resisted simplified reductions in comparing different phenomena, as he favoured a generalised perception that sees in each and every act of reform a potential for the pervasive tendencies of the will to power to spread through the cracks of minimal resistance. As an example, Vidler states that in the case of the OMA's Arnhem prison, the new scheme could be seen as a simple displacement of one form of power with another, the cross instead of the circle, without the production of an effective change internally.

OMA's later competition scheme for the reconstruction of Tate Modern on London's South Bank (1994) expressed a similar gesture in proposing to abolish the old station's landmark tower. Aimed as an act against the system of values where the tower stands for the power of observation and control, OMA's proposal was perceived as insensitive and too literal. This led to Herzog and De Meuron winning the competition.

To conclude this chapter I need to mention Paul Hirst's work again, as it epitomises the works in architectural history and theory that have emerged in the last two decades. In *Space and Power: Politics, War and Architecture* (2005), Hirst states that his book is concerned with space as configured by power, in which space itself becomes the source of power. He argues that space is a resource for power and that thus it makes sense to investigate not 'space' in general, but rather systems of 'space-power' co-relation (Hirst 2005: 3).

Hirst states that his book is concerned with space as configured by power, in which space itself becomes the source of power. He argues that space is a resource for power and that thus it makes sense to investigate not 'space' in general, but rather systems of 'space-power' co-relation.

Hirst stipulates that space is more than the set of co-ordinates in the service of power, as spaces have characteristics that affect the conditions under which power is exercised and where social control and conflicts take place.

Foucault-inspired critique by Hirst operates on three spatial scales: on the level of the state, on the level of the city and on the level of the building as an instrument of power. In the course of his investigation, Hirst identifies three themes: the persistence of forms of exclusive and territorial governance, the role of various kinds of frontiers in different political systems, and the persistence of spatial and material constraints on communication and social action.

Hirst points out that Foucault's best work builds out from an account of particular circumstances. According to Hirst, in analysing concrete spaces of building types Foucault provided a model that unravelled the dynamics of the power-knowledge concept, thus enabling us to think and to understand the structural logic of the effects of spaces such as prisons, hospitals, churches, schools, factories and enclosures in general. Hirst extended his analysis into studying fortification and military structures, due to his interest in the Annales School and his re-examination of the traditional historiography of architecture along the lines of Marx and Nietzsche (Hirst 2005: 4).

Importantly, Hirst needs to be credited for bringing Foucault's discourse into architectural education, as he lectured on Foucault's philosophy and historiography from the early 1980s onwards at the Architectural Association for more than two decades. His inspiring lectures on Foucault alongside those by Mark Cousins, which also tackled the context of the left in France and England in the 1960s and 1970s, shaped the approaches of many graduate students who studied at the AA History and Theory Programme and later taught, practised and lectured worldwide. Geoffrey London, William Taylor, Nader Tehrani, Veronique Parent and Ines Weizman are just a few amongst many that could be named.

# CHAPTER 4

# Bodies

## 4.1 The History of Sexuality

The work on the subject of sexuality was conceived as an extension to the genealogy of discipline and control in society. Foucault's main aim was to problematise the concept of sexuality as it appeared in the nineteenth century. Sexuality, for Foucault, neededs to be reviewed critically in parallel with other phenomena of the time such as the emerging distinction between the fields of knowledge and the establishment of norms that led to the transformations of mentalities and manners in which individuals evaluate their conduct.

More precisely, Foucault aimed to determine the way in which it was possible in Western societies to establish an 'experience' that caused the individuals to recognise themselves as subjects of 'sexuality'. Having completed books on human sciences, psychiatry, medicine and penality, Foucault had the tools required for this critical study, where the experience was analysed in respect to many fields of life (Foucault 1987a: 4).

Foucault's approach was based on his apprehension that various commentaries on sexuality, including psychoanalysis, were related to the exercise of power. He outlined the overall project by demonstrating how modern control of sexuality simultaneously offered knowledge and domination. However, he argued, this control is exercised not only via others' knowledge of individuals; by means of this knowledge, individuals also exercise control over themselves, as they internalise the norms put forward by the theories of sexuality and observe themselves in an effort to conform.

He outlined the overall project by demonstrating how modern control of sexuality simultaneously offered knowledge and domination. However, he argued, this control is exercised not only via others' knowledge of individuals; by means of this knowledge, individuals also exercise control over themselves, as they internalise the norms put forward by the theories of sexuality and observe themselves in an effort to conform.

In keeping with his previous works, Foucault observed that life in the early-seventeenth century was reasonably relaxed about sexuality and that it was only during the eighteenth and nineteenth century that sexuality came under scrutiny. As a result, sexuality gradually became a matter almost exclusive to the conjugal couple, confined to the family home, where the parental bedroom became its official space. The approved behaviour meant avoiding contact with other bodies. Chastity was reflected in language that adhered to similar rules of decorum. Brothels and mental asylums were tolerated, but they were always elsewhere, belonging to the 'other Victorians'. Sex had a right to exist in the invisible places only, in 'clandestine, circumscribed, and coded types of discourse' (Foucault 1987a: 4–5).

While the contribution of twentieth-century discourses such as psychoanalysis has been relevant to the history of sexuality, it is nevertheless, in Foucault's view, limited. He believed that more remained to be grasped and undertaken including the change and transformation of laws, the lifting of prohibitions, the liberation of speech, the reintroduction of pleasures in everyday life and a whole new economy in respect to the mechanisms of power (Foucault 1987a: 5). This range of necessities required a political will and a clear programme, which still eludes us, Foucault concluded.

## *Paradox of repression*

Foucault's critique of sexuality does not aim to save sexuality from being repressed as it is usually thought. Instead, in what came to be known as his 'repressive hypothesis', he exposes as strange the nature of discourse on sexuality and its alleged repression. Foucault demonstrates that sexual discourse has emerged as a mixture of discourses overlaid with power relations, which cannot be clearly understood as repressed.

His analysis distances the discourse of sexuality from the theme of repression by questioning the underlying assumption about the inevitable link between sexual liberation, social freedom and political revolution, as he feels that too many aspirations have been mixed up and put together. Related to this, Foucault aims to uncover the circumstances of the belief that links the discourse on sexuality and the revelation of truth. Equally, he aims to find out more about the supposition about the connection between the overturning of the law and the proclamation of a new and happy life. Foucault points out that the claim about the link between repression, the condemnation of hypocrisy and the approval of the rights of the immediate, has made people project unrealistic hopes about sexual liberation (Foucault 1987a: 8).

Foucault points out that the claim about the link between repression, the condemnation of hypocrisy and the approval of the rights of the immediate, has made people project unrealistic hopes about sexual liberation.

Foucault highlights the strangeness of the claim that sexuality has been the subject of repression precisely at the time when it was coming into prominence and gaining affirmation. He finds this insincere and concludes that the statement about the oppression of sexuality and the 'sermon' about it in fact paradoxically and crucially reinforce each other.

Foucault highlights the strangeness of the claim that sexuality has been the subject of repression precisely at the time when it was coming into prominence and gaining affirmation. He finds this insincere and concludes that the statement about the oppression of sexuality and the 'sermon' about it in fact paradoxically and crucially reinforce each other.

In that sense, Foucault states that the society has been absurdly condemning itself for falseness and silence for over a century, while in fact describing details about 'the things it does not say'. In doing so, the society has been strangely denouncing the power it has exercised in an attempt to apparently liberate itself from the very laws that make it function (Foucault 1987a: 8).

Consequently, Foucault's question is not 'Why are we repressed?' but rather, 'Why do we say with so much passion (against the reality of our past and our present) that we are repressed?' Foucault asks how we came to think that this is the case. Do mechanisms of power such as prohibition, censorship and denial truly belong to the repression of sexuality? Does the critical discourse that addresses repression work against the repression or is it in fact part of it?

In answering these questions, Foucault points out that the nineteenth-century science of sex (*scientia sexualis*) refused to deal openly with its own subject – sex – while addressing its supposed aberrations, perversions and oddities. In that sense, the 'sexual science' spoke solely either on oddities from the moral perspective of the bourgeoisie or on the emerging medical norm based upon the concerns about public health. These two discourses, Foucault argues, did not talk to each other and did not reach the 'truth about sex' either. If anything, it was as if this sexual science tried to prevent any true rational knowledge about sex from emerging.

In that sense, the 'sexual science' spoke solely either on

oddities from the moral perspective of the bourgeoisie or on

the emerging medical norm based upon the concerns about

public health. These two discourses, Foucault argues, did not

talk to each other and did not reach the 'truth about sex'

either. If anything, it was as if this sexual science tried to

prevent any true rational knowledge about sex from emerging.

Foucault describes the status of the nineteenth-century medical practice as
unsubtle, more subordinated to the political powers than to the pursuit of
truth. The emerging social discourse on hygiene, helped by a general fear of
spreading venereal diseases, had grounded the discourse on sexuality within
the concerns of purity, morality and social cleanliness. The politics of sex that
was thus pursued in the nineteenth century relied on the four 'lines of attack'
that combined both discipline and regulatory methods: 1) requirements for
regulation; 2) the sexualisation of children achieved through the form of a
campaign for the health of the species; 3) the hysterisation of women which
Foucault defined as mechanism of power that centres on female body as being
saturated by sex and therefore in need of medicalisation for the reasons of
children's health; and 4) the psychiatrisation of perversions (Foucault 1987a:
146–7).

Foucault determines that by claiming to act in the name of 'truth', this discourse and practice have often cast out the 'defective' or 'degenerate' individuals to various forms of exclusion and racism (1987a: 54). The scientific status of sexuality understood in this way is deeply problematic: it is an uneasy mix of biological knowledge of reproduction and of medicine of sexual pathology.

In support of his hypothesis, Foucault sheds light on the conditions in Jean-Martin Charcot's (1825–93) practice in the Salpêtrière hospital in Paris, which became an enormous apparatus for observation, examination, interrogation and experiment. He shows that the hospital was equally a machinery for incitement, with its public presentations, its theatre of carefully staged ritual crises, its interplay of dialogues, of holding hands between patients and staff, and so on. Foucault argues that it was in this charged and thrilling atmosphere of stimulation to discourse and truth that the mechanism of understanding sexuality operated and made sex a matter of scientific truth and falsehood (Foucault 1987a: 55).

Foucault argues that it was in this charged and thrilling atmosphere of stimulation to discourse and truth that the mechanism of understanding sexuality operated and made sex a matter of scientific truth and falsehood.

### Confession, truth and sex

There have been two essential procedures for producing the truth about sex: 1) *ars erotica*, 'erotic art' as practiced in China, Japan, India, ancient Rome and the Arab/Muslim societies, which was based on individual experience of pleasure and not on an absolute law; and 2) *scientia sexualis*, based on law. It was the latter that prevailed in the predominantly Christian Western world. Foucault argues that the Western science of sexuality as identified in the nineteenth century was founded on the procedures for telling the truth that had developed centuries before. These procedures have their own power / knowledge economy and are based on the confession – a spiritual exercise established in the Middle Ages.

While investigating the genealogy of sexuality, Foucault studied the protocols of confession within Christianity, the demographic discourses of the eighteenth and nineteenth centuries and the medical analysis of sexuality. The unearthing of the centrality of confession for the overall epistemology of Western culture is one of Foucault's chief contributions to knowledge. He argued that confession has been in the heart of Western societies throughout the centuries and that it permeated and affected all aspects of our existence: justice, medicine, education, family relations, love relations and everyday life. The emergence of confession led to a change in the fundamental way of our thinking and theorising in search of the truth. The pursuit of truth was no longer based on seeing, as in ancient Greek *theorein* (θεωρεῖν), to see, it became founded upon *confession* – acknowledgment of one's faith in one's experience of life (ultimately as given by God). This essential shift can explain a number of fundamental changes from the pre-Christian past. It was central to Foucault's turn towards the exploration of late Antiquity.

While investigating the genealogy of sexuality, Foucault studied the protocols of confession within Christianity, the demographic discourses of the eighteenth and nineteenth centuries and the medical analysis of sexuality. The unearthing of the centrality of confession for the overall epistemology of Western culture is one of Foucault's chief contributions to knowledge.

Foucault states that confession is always self-examination. It is through self-examination, which produces a multitude of short-lived and transitory impressions, that one is to invoke the basic certainties of one's consciousness about life. The need to confess by digging into our lives is embedded in our culture and we no longer perceive it as an act of power that pushes us. It appears to us as natural that something such as 'truth' could be perceived as sitting deeply within us. Consequently, argued Foucault, this truth demands one thing – to come to the surface. For a Christian, a confession is a technique that frees; it is the opposite of power that reduces individuals to silence.

The recognition that sex has been a privileged theme of confession within Christianity did not instigate Foucault to think that it was thus necessarily hidden; rather, he thought, it could be that it was important and not forgotten. Foucault recalls that in ancient Greece, truth and sex were linked, in the form of pedagogy, where 'by the transmission of a precarious knowledge from one body to another *sex* served as a *medium* for initiation into learning' (1987a: 61). This was different from what happened later with Christianity, argues Foucault, where truth and sex became joined together through the obligatory practice of confession. But this time, in contrast to Antiquity, it is truth that served as a medium for the manifestations of sex.

Foucault recalls that in ancient Greece, truth and sex were linked, in the form of pedagogy, where 'by the transmission of a precarious knowledge from one body to another *sex* served as a *medium* for initiation into learning'. This was different from what happened later with Christianity, argues Foucault, where truth and sex became joined together through the obligatory practice of confession. But this time, in contrast to Antiquity, it is truth that served as a medium for the manifestations of sex.

According to Foucault, the ritual discourse of confession opens up knowledge within a setting of power relations. It is so because one always confesses to somebody who is an authority and who intervenes in order to judge, punish, forgive, console or reconcile. Through the ceremony of confession, the person changes, as confessing produces intrinsic modifications in the person who articulates it:

> ... it exonerates, redeems, and purifies him; it unburdens him of wrongs, liberates him, and promises him salvation (Foucault 1987a: 62).

Confession lends itself to the new domains and explorations. It is not simply about recounting what happened in the sexual act, but rather about the analysis, reconstruction and description, including the accompanied thoughts and fantasies, the recollection of images, desires and aspects of pleasure.

The deployment of confession in the nineteenth-century science of sexuality led Foucault to conclude that the society had for the first time and under the guise of pragmatic concerns for public health taken it upon itself to solicit and to hear about individual private pleasure (Foucault 1987a: 63). In doing so, it multiplied and intensified its own incentives to knowledge and its own intrinsic pleasures, thus functioning as an *ars erotica*. In this way, a new kind of pleasure was formed: the pleasure in the truth of pleasure, the pleasure of knowing that truth, the pleasure of analysis itself (1987a: 71). The complex interplay between knowledge, truth, power and pleasure is here even more complex.

In this way, a new kind of pleasure was formed: the pleasure in the truth of pleasure, the pleasure of knowing that truth, the pleasure of analysis itself.

### Blood and the symbolic vs sexuality and the norm

Foucault makes a comparison between the past societies that placed importance and value on blood relations and present societies. He analysed how blood relations remained for a long time an important element in the manifestation and rituals of power. In societies where there was a constant threat from famine, epidemics and violence, one can see the reasons why blood constituted one of its fundamental values. During the classical age, this changed, according to Foucault. He explains how the new procedures of power that were devised and gradually employed during the late-eighteenth and nineteenth century caused our societies to transform their dominant organisational paradigm from a symbolic of blood to an analytic of sexuality (1987a: 148). He argued that while blood was implicated in relation to the law, death, transgression, the symbolic and sovereignty, sexuality was on the side of the norm, knowledge, life, meaning, disciplines and regulations.

In societies where there was a constant threat from famine, epidemics and violence, one can see the reasons why blood constituted one of its fundamental values. During the classical age, this changed, according to Foucault. He explains how the new procedures of power that were devised and gradually employed during the late-eighteenth and nineteenth century caused our societies to transform their dominant organisational paradigm from a symbolic of blood to an analytic of sexuality.

Within architectural history, we can observe the same two strands of relations and their hierarchies. There has been a particular architecture related to the aspects of life dictated by blood relations, addressing explicitly features and phenomena of life such as death, the symbolic, transgression, the law and sovereignty. This architecture relates to the edifices of Antiquity and of the

Middle Ages stretching up until the seventeenth century. We read about its ancient examples in Alberti's *De re aedificatoria* (1452). However, this architecture of mythic origins, fratricide, sacrifice, cosmology, the old and the new Babylons and Romes, rulers, airs and blood was gradually replaced by another kind of architecture – the architecture of the norm, knowledge, meaning and regulations as we know it from the nineteenth century onwards and as embraced by and large by the Modern Movement.

Equally important is Foucault's point that radical phenomena such as racism emerged in the nineteenth century, when the concerns for the politics of settlement, family, hygiene, social hierarchy and property (accompanied by a series of interventions at the level of the body, conduct, health, and so on) gained ground, ultimately leading to their extreme form in Nazism (Foucault 1987a: 149).

### 4.2 Sexuality, knowledge and the structure of aesthetic experience

The commitment to capture poignant arguments about sexuality and its history was central to Foucault's work. This included the close reading of the traditional philosophy of the ancient world, pursued during the philosopher's final years. Foucault's concern was that any grasp of Christian morality required a comparison with ancient understandings of the ethical self. This led him to the finding that sexuality, ethics and knowledge in antiquity were inextricably linked within the structure of the aesthetic experience.

This led him to the finding that sexuality, ethics and knowledge in antiquity were inextricably linked within the structure of the aesthetic experience.

Foucault contrasted the predominantly nineteenth-century Victorian view, in which sexual acts were seen as problematic, with the Greek understanding that perceived sexual activity as good, natural and necessary, though potentially subject to abuse. He was interested in comparing the way in which the ancients paid attention to the proper use of pleasures (*chresis*), which included various sexual activities such as heterosexual, homosexual, marital and extra-marital, all taken in moderation, with Christian morality, which argued predominantly for abstention. Foucault problematised notions such as freedom and truth within the context of sexuality. He referred to the ancient question about whether or not a man devoted to pleasures could be truly free (Foucault 1987b: 78).

Foucault disengaged the ancient notion of *sophrosyne* (self-mastery, which included sexual restraint) from the Christian understanding of restraint linked to purity. He stated that the ancient Greeks did not believe that they would be able to regain innocence or maintain purity simply by sexual abstention. They practiced restraint in order to remain free. For the ancients, moderation or self-rule was the ability required to rule over others (Foucault 1987b: 78–82).

Foucault disengaged the ancient notion of *sophrosyne* (self-mastery, which included sexual restraint) from the Christian understanding of restraint linked to purity. He stated that the ancient Greeks did not believe that they would be able to regain innocence or maintain purity simply by sexual abstention.

Foucault problematised the fact that moderation was perceived as essentially male and 'virile'. This did not mean that women were not capable of *sophrosyne*; however, this virtue would be linked to virility and to their relation to man. As a consequence of this structure, where moderation was understood as masculine, immoderation was seen as related to femininity (1987b: 82).

Foucault argued that the freedom / power duality, which characterised the life of moderate (and righteous) men, was necessarily linked to truth. According to Aristotle, to rule one's pleasures and to bring them under the authority of *logos* formed one and the same undertaking. The necessary link between wisdom and moderation meant that one could not practise moderation without certain knowledge. As Foucault put it, 'One could not form oneself as an ethical subject in the use of pleasures without forming oneself at the same time as a subject of knowledge' (1987b: 86).

The necessary link between wisdom and moderation meant that one could not practise moderation without certain knowledge. As Foucault put it, 'One could not form oneself as an ethical subject in the use of pleasures without forming oneself at the same time as a subject of knowledge'.

### Desire, love and truth

In order to shed more light on the life of the ancients, Foucault discusses love and knowledge with reference to the themes from Plato's *Phaedrus*, where 'the drama of the soul is struggling with itself against the drama of its desires' (Foucault 1987b). He points out how the relationship to truth emerges in the state of love as recognition of a long-lost beauty.

Foucault concludes that for the ancients, the relation to truth was therefore a structural, instrumental and ontological condition for establishing moderation. It is not solely a matter of individuals being able to recognise the forbidden and purify themselves of the desire that was brought to light. Moderation was an aesthetic matter – part of the aesthetics of existence, whose moral value depended on, amongst other things, certain formal principles in the use of pleasures, in regards to their limits and their hierarchy (1987b: 89).

Moderation was guided by common sense about the appropriateness of behaviour in respect to needs, time and standing. The *ascesis* (i.e. the restraint in worldly pleasures in the pursuit of salvation or liberation) that the individual was undertaking, Foucault argued, had a form of a personal struggle in order to establish the power of self-mastery. Experienced as active freedom, it was inseparable from its structural relation to the truth (Foucault 1987b: 92).

Moderation was an aesthetic matter – part of the aesthetics of existence, whose moral value depended on, amongst other things, certain formal principles in the use of pleasures, in regards to their limits and their hierarchy.

The finding that the ancient Greeks and Romans understood sexuality and moderation, neither through the codification of acts nor through the interpretation of desire but through an aesthetic experience, is important for Foucault. So is the understanding that sex was both a pleasure and a necessary part of an aesthetic life, which individuals create for themselves.

The finding that the ancient Greeks and Romans understood sexuality and moderation, neither through the codification of acts nor through the interpretation of desire but through an aesthetic experience, is important for Foucault.

This recognition confirms Foucault's understanding of ancient Greek philosophy's being a way of life that strives towards a good and beautiful existence (*bene e beato vivere*). This attitude contrasts with the traditional Western understanding of philosophy as a search for philosophical truth and the subsequent Protestant ideology of life centred on work.

*Speaking truthfully*

Although Foucault began his discussion on Plato's philosophy in *The Use of Pleasure*, his more detailed attention to this subject came in his 1980s lectures at the Collège de France, including the 1981–2 course entitled 'The Hermeneutics of the Subject', which had Plato's *Alcibiades* as its point of departure (2005: 25–43). In these lectures, Foucault focused on the 'care of the self', commenting on writers such as Epictetus, Seneca and Plutarch, and addressing the relationship between the care of the self, the politics of the city, defective pedagogy and self-knowledge.

Foucault addresses the ancient ideal of 'truthful speech' (*parrhesia*), regarded as the central political and moral virtue, by examining earlier formulations of the notion in Euripides and Socrates as well as its later transformations by the Epicureans, Stoics and Cynics. Based on traditional philosophy and on an essay by Georges Dumézil that addressed the death of Socrates, Foucault shows how *parrhesia* and the 'care of the self' can guide us to the truth of ourselves. The main issue is to address the conditions that lead to the type of human conduct where what is required is not only to obey but also to reveal what one is. Foucault studied penitence and the examination of consciousness in monasteries (which included the duty to tell everything about oneself to the 'master'), concluding that the medieval practice of confession was a modified form of the ancient 'technique of the self' (Foucault 1987a: 58–61).

Based on traditional philosophy and on an essay by Georges Dumézil that addressed the death of Socrates, Foucault shows how *parrhesia* and the 'care of the self' can guide us to the truth of ourselves. The main issue is to address the conditions that lead to the type of human conduct where what is required is not only to obey but also to reveal what one is.

By making reference to Galen (129–c. 200), a well-known physician and philosopher, Foucault argues about the individual's need to constantly exert oneself to oneself. It is a particular trope – a turn of the soul to itself – and as such, argues Foucault, it is also 'a kind of turning back to light, to reality, to the divine, to essences, to the super-celestial'. It is also about 'turning around on the spot' and ultimately 'turning oneself to oneself and staying there' (Foucault 1983). In doing so, Foucault argues, getting rid of bad pedagogy and its damage is important for acquiring new knowledge, as one often has to consciously 'unlearn' in order to be able to learn something else – a point not to be forgotten in the context of architectural education.

### Crisis, self and finitude

While working on these complex and sensitive subjects in 1979, Foucault swapped the busy and overcrowded Bibliothèque Nationale for another study venue – the library of the Dominican order in Paris, the Bibliothèque du Saulchoir, in Rue de la Glacière in the thirteenth arrondissment. This point is of interest as evidence towards Foucault's own psycho-geography. In the new setting, which became his permanent study place, Foucault worked in a small reading room as the guest of Michel Alabric, the monk and the Director of the Saulchoir. Foucault cherished this relationship and has argued that the monastic life appealed to him and that were it not for his atheism, he could have lived happily as a monk (Macey 2004: 129–30).

Foucault explored the care of the self when he was going through a process of reflection about his own life. He contemplated leaving Collège and giving up writing, admitting that writing was not something he had consciously planned or chosen. His close friend Hervé Guibert recalls how the last two volumes of *The History of Sexuality* were written and rewritten, destroyed, disowned, rethought, shortened and lengthened over almost a decade and how Foucault called it a book 'of doubt, of rebirth' and 'of grandiose modesty' (Guibert 1988; Eribon 1993: 322).

Nevertheless, the two books came out aiming to profoundly excavate and decode the birth of the modern individual and the formation of his or her self-consciousness. The style of these volumes is different; the tone is pacified and, according to Blanchot, the words are calmer and appeased (Blanchot 1987; Eribon 1993: 331). The works of Seneca were amongst Foucault's favourite readings, while his whole life gradually became one of peace and stoicism. It was as if he adopted the ancient wisdom concerning the 'stylization of existence'. Driven not by any kind of historicity, it was, as Deleuze has pointed out, motivated by the concerns for 'us today' (Deleuze 1986). In Foucault's own words:

**What strikes me is the fact that in our society, art has become something which is related only to objects and not to individuals or to life... But could not everyone's life become a work of art? (Dreyfus and Rabinow 1982: 237)**

The works of Seneca were amongst Foucault's favourite readings, while his whole life gradually became one of peace and stoicism. It was as if he adopted the ancient wisdom concerning the 'stylization of existence'. Driven not by any kind of historicity, it was, as Deleuze has pointed out, motivated by the concerns for 'us today'.

'What strikes me is the fact that in our society, art has become something which is related only to objects and not to individuals or to life... But could not everyone's life become a work of art?'

In the last lecture delivered at the Collège in 1982, Foucault made reference to Stoic teachings. He argued that meditation on death has particular value, because it anticipates what is generally considered as the greatest misfortune and makes it possible to convince oneself that death is not an evil. According to Foucault, this meditation also

Michel Foucault lecturing at the Collège de France (1974–1975).

**offers the possibility of casting, in anticipation so to speak, a backward glance on life. In considering oneself as on the point of dying, one can judge each of the acts that one is in the process of committing according to its own worth (Foucault 1989: 165–6).**

The discussion about the individual's care of the self became even more prominent towards the end of Foucault's life. Undertaken with the awareness of various historical forces (organic, economic and linguistic) operating upon an individual human life, Foucault's discussion on finitude is philosophical as well as personal. As he argued, the same experiential and historically limited human being is always both the reflecting individual and the source of his or her own knowledge.

In this constellation, the consciousness must be both an empirical object of representation and the source of understanding. Foucault sketches the historical case for this discussion, which he called the 'analytic of finitude', understood as thinking about the conditions that make us finite (our subjection to space, time, causality and so on), which are also the conditions that take part in our thinking, which as such are necessary for the possibility of knowledge (Foucault 1989). Our finitude is, therefore, simultaneously founded and founding (positive and fundamental, as Foucault puts it). This shows that man must be viewed as irreducibly empirical and transcendental, where neither can be suppressed.

Given the empirical and historical understanding of who we are, Foucault argues that the problem is that the modern notion of man excludes Descartes's idea of the cogito as a 'sovereign transparency' of pure consciousness. Thought is no longer pure representation and therefore cannot be separated from an 'unthought'. We cannot equalise the content of 'I think' to the content of 'I am', because the content of the subject's reality is always more than the content of any merely thinking self. The fact is that individuals are living, working, desiring and speaking subjects: these conditions take any individual beyond the realm of mere thought (Foucault 1989: 165–6).

We cannot equalise the content of 'I think' to the content of 'I am', because the content of the subject's reality is always more than the content of any merely thinking self. The fact is that individuals are living, working, desiring and speaking subjects: these conditions take any individual beyond the realm of mere thought.

## 4.3 Biopower

This concept first emerged in Volume 1 of *The History of Sexuality,* when Foucault identified that within the new welfare agenda of the nineteenth century, sexuality became central to the administration of the conditions of life (Foucault 1987a: 133–61). Foucault observed two strands to this development: the first is linked to the disciplinary institutions such as the army, schools and related discourses; and the second is about the emergence of demographics, the analysis of population, wealth and resources. These two separate strands of practices and discourses were joined through the set of arrangements that would produce the great technology of power in the nineteenth century with the deployment of sexuality being one of the key arrangements (Foucault 1987a: 140).

Echoing the works of Marx and Engels, Foucault argues that biopower was indispensable in the development of capitalism. However, it is not that bodies only need to be 'inserted into' the process of production; the society also requires growth of the production and of population, as well as their availability and docility.

Echoing the works of Marx and Engels, Foucault argues that biopower was indispensable in the development of capitalism. However, it is not that bodies only need to be 'inserted into' the process of production; the society also requires growth of the production and of population, as well as their availability and docility. The institutions and businesses ensure production processes, while the techniques of power operate on the individual, the family, the school and the army (Foucault 1987a: 141). It was biopower that adjusted the accumulation of men to capital, joining the growth of human groups to the expansion of productive forces. Architecture was vital in facilitating this process of managing docility and production, as both had to be distributed in space.

It was biopower that adjusted the accumulation of men to capital, joining the growth of human groups to the expansion of productive forces. Architecture was vital in facilitating this process of managing docility and production, as both had to be distributed in space.

In this context, Foucault notes an aspect that was rarely appreciated, which he described as 'nothing less than the entry of life into history' (Foucault 1987a: 141). By this, he means that in the eighteenth century, when economic development and its increased productivity became more rapid than the growth of the population, a certain release from the traditional pressures of famine and epidemics was achieved. This newly gained relative control of life provided for new views upon life. Foucault wrote,

**Western man was gradually learning what it meant to be a living species in a living world, to have a body, conditions of existence, probabilities of life, an individual and collective welfare, forces that could be modified, and a space in which they could be distributed in an optimal manner (Foucault 1987a: 142).**

In this new mode of viewing the relation between history and life, people were able to see life in its dual position, argues Foucault, 'placed within its biological environment outside history, and at the same time inside human historicity, equipped with history's techniques of knowledge and power'. The political technologies have gradually been applied to life, to bodies, to related issues such as health, living conditions, habitation and architecture, and to the whole space of existence, including planning of the urban, rural and open spaces of landscape (Foucault 1987a: 142).

## The political technologies have gradually been applied to life, to bodies, to related issues such as health, living conditions, habitation and architecture, and to the whole space of existence, including planning of the urban, rural and open spaces of landscape.

Foucault tells us that sexuality in the nineteenth century became an important field for biopower because it was linking two separate domains of life: the disciplines of the body and the regulations of population. He observed that sexuality fitted both categories at once, on the one hand giving rise to endless 'surveillances, permanent controls, extremely meticulous orderings of space, indeterminate medical or psychological examinations, to an entire micro-power concerned with the body', while on the other addressing the state of the nation's body – its population (Foucault 1987a: 145–6).

### Norm, body, fashion and related arts

One of the main consequences of the emergence of biopower, argues Foucault, was the rise of norms at the expense of the juridical system of the law. Ideally, norms distribute conditions of life in an optimal fashion for the maintenance of life without privileges. The power that takes charge of life needs continuous, regulatory and corrective mechanisms, as it is about distributing the living beings into the domain of value and utility. The normative function that emerges is thus able to

> **qualify, measure, appraise, and hierarchize, rather than display itself in its murderous splendour; it does not have to draw the line that separates the enemies of the sovereign from his obedient subjects; it effects distributions around the norm (Foucault 1987a: 144).**

The power that takes charge of life needs continuous, regulatory

and corrective mechanisms, as it is about distributing the living

beings into the domain of value and utility.

In parallel to the establishment of norm and normativity, the law or the institutions of justice did not entirely disappear. During this process and as a consequence, the law itself began to operate as a norm, while judicial institutions became incorporated into the state apparatuses (e.g. medical, administrative, educational and so on) whose functions became regulatory. In that sense, Foucault concludes, normalising society and its normative mechanisms are the historical outcomes of the technology of power as exercised in Europe. The process can be seen as a regression, as it essentially and irreversibly made the normalising power acceptable.

In that sense, Foucault concludes, normalising society and its normative mechanisms are the historical outcomes of the technology of power as exercised in Europe. The process can be seen as a regression, as it essentially and irreversibly made the normalising power acceptable.

Driven by the need to maintain the biopower, the process of proliferation of norms had numerous consequences. On the level of the subject, what was demanded was the 'right' to life, to one's body, to health, to happiness and to the satisfaction of needs, and beyond all oppression or 'alienation', the 'right' to rediscover what one is and what one can be. Foucault argues that the ancient regime and the classical age were not able to comprehend this 'right', which was the political response to the new context of the different power procedures (Foucault 1987a: 145).

This process extended to the practices of architecture, interior design, development of fashion and the establishment of taste. Because Foucault's approach radically analysed body and space, it is useful in tracing the development of architecture and other related crafts. In the field of interior design and fashion, the developments in French furniture and couture emerged as part of the same historical phenomenon, as they endorsed the new relationship to human body.

Indeed fashion (la mode) could be traced back to Versailles, its courtiers and their clothing that emerged under the reign of Louis XIV, when the luxury-goods industries came under royal jurisdiction and the royal court became the arbiter of taste and style in France. The rise of French fashion in the 1670s, during what Foucault called the 'classical period', exemplifies the rise of another state-led, body-controlling institution under the auspices of the king. This fashion was supported by the related discourse that emerged in the literary, arts and society magazines such as the gazette *Le Mercure galant*, founded in 1672 by Jean Donneau de Visé. These fashion ideas, together with designs and garments, were exported outside France, as most European monarchs were willing to emulate the style of the French king.

The rise of French fashion in the 1670s, during what Foucault called the 'classical period', exemplifies the rise of another state-led, body-controlling institution under the auspices of the king. This fashion was supported by the related discourse that emerged in the literary, arts and society magazines such as the gazette *Le Mercure galant*, founded in 1672 by Jean Donneau de Visé.

Observed 'structurally', the old ways of clothing the body based on veiling and folding were no longer perceived as satisfactory. The cuts (*couture*) became more prominent and central to the new approach to clothing the body. The relation to the human figure required not simply luxury but mastery and a more precise and supportive structure for the garments.

Observed 'structurally', the old ways of clothing the body based on veiling and folding were no longer perceived as satisfactory. The cuts (*couture*) became more prominent and central to the new approach to clothing the body.

Fashion acquired a different critical input from the normative realm after the French bourgeois revolution. The new way of cutting fabric into anatomically determined, body-parts-related pieces that developed in the eighteenth and nineteenth centuries was more functional. Even today, we can observe how these specific cuts continue to mark the European style of couture and clothing, when compared to fashion garments from outside Europe. This underlying condition of the ways dresses were made is therefore one of the effects of the normative approach taken towards clothing the body.

Fashion acquired a different critical input from the normative realm after the French bourgeois revolution. The new way of cutting fabric into anatomically determined, body-parts-related pieces that developed in the eighteenth and nineteenth centuries was more functional.

Another parallel could be found in relation to interiors and the emergence of furniture and cabinet making, as they became defined in relation to the body and the norm. The definition of elements for sitting, sleeping or storing, in the form of armchairs, beds or storage, set the fashion, standard and definitions that remain in use even today, despite modernism's apparently radical design proposals. Even the latest designers continue to produce furnishings such as commodes, chaise-longues, semainiers, fauteuils and other types of furniture that have persisted within the European cabinet-making industry.

## Taste

The new attitude towards knowledge, control and life that has embraced the norm as grasped by Foucault, and as evident in arts, crafts and fashion, unfolded in relation to the emergence of *taste* – an eighteenth-century category. Since then, the discourse on taste in the matters of environment, clothing, furnishing interiors and designing buildings has remained central to the history of European culture. The eighteenth-century philosophical discourse on aesthetics is the effect of these new phenomena and emerging categories. Although Foucault did not address the arts, fashion and architecture as presented here, his work invites us to contemplate them in this manner. These issues and wider aspects, including the relationship between a sense of taste and of power, and how material reality came to dominate the sense of taste, could be explored further.

The eighteenth-century philosophical discourse on aesthetics is the effect of these new phenomena and emerging categories. Although Foucault did not address the arts, fashion and architecture as presented here, his work invites us to contemplate them in this manner. These issues and wider aspects, including the relationship between a sense of taste and of power, and how material reality came to dominate the sense of taste, could be explored further.

It is fascinating to observe how Foucault's volumes of *The History of Sexuality* opened up not one argument nor a series of arguments but several series of arguments, by beginning with a single question that challenged the widely held opinion about sexuality and its presumed repression. One of these series of arguments relates to the critical revision of the development of public space and the city in respect to the new discourse on body.

### 4.4 Bodies, architecture and cities

Foucault discussed the development of rationality in architecture as a function of the aims and techniques of the governments from the eighteenth century onwards. It was at this time, he argued, that the governmental discourse on order emerged, addressing what the order of the society should be and what the cities ought to be like. More specifically, Foucault contended, every treatise on politics from then onwards included chapters on urbanism, collective facilities, hygiene and private architecture (Foucault 1991b: 239).

Foucault believed that the architectural discourse of his time began to acknowledge the duality between the building and its space and to recognise the latter. Throughout the modern period up until the 1980s, architects considered that their main task was to design *built forms*. Although it is not always transparently clear, it was in part due to Foucault and his followers that architects shifted focus from concerns about the built form to the design of *space itself*. Crucially, Foucault demonstrated that this space is not neutral or empty but a space of social relations. He recognised the role of architecture in allocating people and in organising various flows of movement within urban contexts – what we might call architecture as exoskeleton. By acting in this way, architecture partakes in the practice of codification of various positions and places which are not neutral but set within the system of power relations. Foucault wrote,

> It is true that for me, architecture, in the very vague analyses... is only taken as an element of support, to ensure a certain allocation of people in space, a *canalization* of their circulation, as well as the coding of their reciprocal relations. So it is not only considered an element in space, but is especially thought of as a *plunge* into a field of social relations in which it brings about some specific effects (Foucault 1991b: 253).

Although it is not always transparently clear, it was in part

due to Foucault and his followers that architects shifted focus

from concerns about the built form to the design of *space*

*itself*. Crucially, Foucault demonstrated that this space is not neutral or empty but a space of social relations. He recognised the role of architecture in allocating people and in organising various flows of movement within urban contexts – what we might call architecture as exoskeleton.

Foucault sees in a number of phenomena the reasons for architecture entering the mind of political men in the seventeenth and the eighteenth century, including the fact that the city became a model for thinking about large states such as France. The plan of Versailles, with its endless, structured gardens that extend and project externally, is a case in point. Importantly, Foucault argued, the eighteenth-century city was no longer perceived as a space of privilege or as an exception in the territory of fields, forests and roads. Instead, he writes,

> ... the cities, with the problems that they raised, and the particular forms that they took, served as the models for the governmental rationality that was to apply to the whole of the territory (Foucault 1991b: 241).

This point discloses at least two things: first, that the balance between the

Foucault's house in Rue Vaugirard, Paris 15th arr.

city and the surrounding territory was changing as the city became larger and significantly different; and second, that the city became a model of rationality and governability for the country, implying that the city was previously not a model of rationality but rather an outgrown whole that needed attention. The mastery over the city was gradually taking place at the end of the seventeenth and beginning of the eighteenth century.

In this respect, Foucault notes that in policing, it was assumed that the state would be well run if its systems of control were as tight and as efficient as the ones of the city. The term 'policing' here refers not simply to the men in uniform but to the overall 'programme of government's rationality'. This is based on a French model that was a project to create 'a system of regulation of the general conduct of individuals whereby everything would be controlled to the point of self-sustenance without the need for intervention' (Foucault 1991b: 241).

We can recognise the important role of the city as it produced the effects upon the state and society on many levels. The notions of inside and outside that previously applied to the city were now becoming applicable to the state (Fontana-Giusti 2011) and the relationships between the states gradually became codified based upon the cities model. The idea of sovereignty and the related concepts such as city walls, now contemplated and defended as state borders, became reinforced, which was noticeable in the rise of the production and proliferation of maps that from the seventeenth century onwards displayed more state borders.

We can recognise the important role of the city as it produced the effects upon the state and society on many levels. The notions of inside and outside that previously applied to the city were now becoming applicable to the state and the relationships between the states gradually became codified based upon the cities model.

## Systems, relations and networks

During the eighteenth and nineteenth centuries, the idea appeared that governability was needed to penetrate, stimulate, regulate and render all the mechanisms within the state. This generated different ideas and responses, where, according to Foucault, one of the main legacies of political thought at the end of the eighteenth century was the idea of *society* itself. By society, he meant the 'complex and independent reality that has its own laws and mechanisms of reaction, its regulations as well as its possibilities of disturbance' (Foucault 1991b: 242).

Foucault highlighted the importance of the nineteenth-century legacy in developing infrastructure by pointing out how the railway network became a significant spatial and political factor. The effects of the railways were revolutionary, as trains provided new connectivity. There were speculations about the effects of increased familiarity among people, including the new possibilities of getting married in a different city and the view that the new universality might make war impossible.

The effects of the railways were revolutionary, as trains provided new connectivity.

Foucault argued that electricity was another similar development that was changing the city, its space and the set of power relations in the nineteenth century. Consequently, he adds, it was the engineers (*polytechniciens*), the builders of bridges and viaducts, roads and railways, who made the space, not the architects. According to Foucault, architects are no longer the main masters of space because they are not the controllers of the three great variables – territory, communication and speed (Foucault 1991b: 242).

Foucault argued that electricity was another similar development that was changing the city, its space and the set of power relations in the nineteenth century. Consequently, he adds, it

was the engineers (*polytechniciens*), the builders of bridges

and viaducts, roads and railways, who made the space, not the

architects. According to Foucault, architects are no longer the

main masters of space because they are not the controllers of the

three great variables – territory, communication and speed.

Regarding the role and the character of architecture, Foucault stated that architectural projects cannot be classified as 'liberal' or 'oppressive'. While there are spaces of oppression, he continued, these places could also be turned into places of resistance and opposition – i.e. there is nothing in the form itself that is functionally liberating. This is due to the fact that liberty is a practice.

While there are projects and buildings that produce specific effects and work through various kinds of constraints, it is not inherent to the structure to be the guarantor of freedom. Architecture can increase its spatial effects when the intentions of the architect coincide with the practice of the users involved. However, neither the intentions of the architect nor the effects of architecture are fundamental. For Foucault, nothing is fundamental in the analysis of society, as there are no fundamental phenomena but 'only reciprocal relations, and the perpetual gaps between intentions in relation to one another' (Foucault 1991b: 247). Architecture functions within this context of reciprocity, gaps and overlap.

However, neither the intentions of the architect nor the

effects of architecture are fundamental. For Foucault, nothing

is fundamental in the analysis of society, as there are no

fundamental phenomena but 'only reciprocal relations, and the perpetual gaps between intentions in relation to one another'.

### Gender studies, sexuality and space

It is impossible to list the full impact of the volumes of *The History of Sexuality*. In the past three decades, societies have acquired a more open approach in regards to issues of gender and sexuality. Although some feminists have rejected Foucault's work, others have explored it. Points of convergence between feminist theory and Foucault's work have been approached in the work of scholars such as Lois McNay (McNay 1994) and Judith Butler (Butler 1990, 2004). McNay argues that feminism has something to gain from the reading of Foucault's work while it also provides a constructive criticism to some of Foucault's limitations (e.g. the possibility to initiate change). Butler's work extended the implications of Foucault's 'repressive hypothesis' into aspects of gender and identity and became an important source of feminism and queer theory. Her argument in *Gender Trouble: Feminism and Subversion of Identity* (1990) states that the apparent coherence of the categories of sex, gender and sexuality – such as heterosexual desire – is culturally constructed through the repetition of acts in time and space. Agreed by convention, these bodily acts establish the appearance of an essential, 'core' gender, which Butler identified as performative. This is not a voluntary choice, Butler argues; she locates the construction of the gendered, sexed, desiring subject within Foucault's critique of normative discourses as argued in *Discipline and Punish* and *The History of Sexuality* Volume 1.

Butler's argument in *Gender Trouble: Feminism and Subversion of Identity* states that the apparent coherence of the categories of sex, gender, and sexuality – such as heterosexual desire – is culturally constructed through the repetition of acts in time and space.

The writers on gender have inspired related discourse in architecture that appeared as critical essays published in volumes such as *Sexuality and Space* (Colomina 1992), *Desiring Practices: Architecture, Gender and the Interdisciplinary* (McCorquodale, Wigglesworth and Ruedi 1996), *Sex and Architecture* (Agrest, Conway, Weisman 1996) and *Negotiating Domesticity: Spatial Productions of Gender in Modern Architecture* (Heynen and Baydar 2005). In these volumes, we read how gender-related discussions entered the realm of architecture and, although it is possible to observe how the tide of these discourses vary, nevertheless it is no longer possible to ignore the gender-related critical agenda. The particular topics differ and can involve subjects ranging from the feminist critique, such as the issues of the excluded femininity and anthropocentricism (Agrest 1996) to the critique of the male-centred articulation of the hierarchy of spaces (Wigley 1992: 345–6).

In 'Untitled: The House of Gender', Mark Wigley specifically addresses Foucault's work in regard to bodies and architecture. Wigley argues that the disciplining of the body was an extension of the traditional disciplining of 'the cultural artefact called woman', authorised by the claim that she was too much a part of the fluid bodily world to be able to control herself (Wigley 1992: 345). By making reference to Foucault, Wigley suggests that the common trait to the arguments about space is that they are instituted to construct the specific set of conditions for the individuals (Wigley 1992: 345–6).

In 'Untitled: The House of Gender', Mark Wigley specifically addresses Foucault's work in regard to bodies and architecture. Wigley argues that the disciplining of the body was an extension of the traditional disciplining of 'the cultural artefact called woman', authorised by the claim that she was too much a part of the fluid bodily world to be able to control herself.

Apart from the works of such architectural theorists as Agrest and Wigley, Foucault-related discussions on gender, sexuality and cities can be found in the works of contemporary critics such as Elizabeth Grosz, Giuliana Bruno and Richard Sennett. For example, in her critical studies on body, space and the city, philosopher and feminist Elizabeth Grosz refers to Foucault when she aims to surpass the oppositions that had governed the traditional discourse on body. She produces a novel reflection on body and the city by bringing in Foucault's notion of 'the micro-technologies of power' and stating that,

> The body is, so to speak, organically/biologically/naturally 'incomplete'; it is indeterminate, amorphous, a series of uncoordinated potentialities which require social triggering, ordering, and long-term 'administration', regulated in each culture and epoch by what Foucault has called 'the micro-technologies of power' (Grosz 1992: 243).

Grosz understands the city as the network which links together in a disintegrated way a number of disparate social activities, processes and relations, with imaginary and real spaces. In grasping this relationship between the body and the city, Grosz draws from *Discipline and Punish* and *The History of Sexuality*, describing mechanisms within the urban culture that are linked to the concept of biopower (Grosz 1992: 241–9).

In *Public Intimacy, Architecture and the Visual Arts* (2007), art historian Giuliana Bruno analyses the notion of public intimacy in a series of essays on art, architecture and public spaces, taking into the account the body that acquired 'an increasing interest in the cultural production of the last three centuries' (Bruno 2007: 102). By exploring architecture as the frame of memory in the context of museum and film studies, Bruno echoes Foucault's discourse on the body:

> Understood as a discourse on the fabric of the body, cinema shares epistemological foundations with the scientific investigation of *corporis fabrica* (Bruno 2007: 102).

Bruno explains how this is both a philosophical and a scientific phenomenon that can be traced back through the genealogy of representational codes. Following Foucault, she explains how medical discourse on the body, which coincided with the invention of cinema, has furthered its use of the gaze as an analytic instrument and advanced the development of visual instruments and techniques which became of relevance for other disciplines (see Chapter 3 of this book, 'The birth of the scientific gaze').

The work of historian Richard Sennett bears a close proximity to Foucault's ideas on sexuality – apparent not only in their joint article, 'Sexuality and Solitude' (Sennett and Foucault 1981) that nevertheless contains their separate parts, but in a wider sense. Sennett remarked that his studies of the human body began with Foucault in the late 1970s and that the French philosopher's influence may be felt throughout *Flesh and Stone,* Sennett's book on the body and the city (Sennett 1994: 26–7). By incorporating into the book the questions of sexuality which he shared with Foucault, Sennett emphasised the awareness of pleasure as well as that of pain. Importantly, based on the reading of Foucault's latter two volumes of *The History of Sexuality* and affected by the manner of Foucault's painful death, Sennett recognised the pain as beyond the reach of the theoretical calculations that he had initially contemplated for his *Flesh and Stone* (Sennett 1994: 27). In this way, by means of contemplation and analysis on Foucault and the body, the depth of the mutual relation between human knowledge and existence came to the fore in Sennett's book on urban life and corporeal experience.

CHAPTER 5

# Spatiality / Aesthetics

### 5.1 Spatiality and its themes of heterogeneity, infinity and spacing out of language

Foucault was an exceptionally visual and 'spatial' writer. His texts are abundant with vivid images that call for theoretical research on spatiality in which seeing, surface and space all have a role. In this final chapter, under 'spatiality' I shall examine this aspect of Foucault's work that in part intersects with his discourse on art and aesthetics. My commentaries will mainly relate to the essay 'On other spaces' (Foucault 1993), *Death and the Labyrinth* (2004), the 'Theatrum Philosophicum' essay in *Language, Counter-memory, Practice* (1977) and selected extracts from the essays in *Aesthetics, Method and Epistemology* (1998) and *Dits et écrits* volume 4 (1994). The theoretical ground of these texts will be addressed in terms of spatial references identifying the change in Foucault's discourse that demonstrates how spatial metaphors from his early works have turned into the discourse on space.

## Foucault's manner of thinking has always been animated and spatial. His thoughts give the impression of unfolding in a three-dimensional display.

Foucault's manner of thinking has always been animated and spatial. His thoughts give the impression of unfolding in a three-dimensional display. The dynamic and direct character of his writing comes from the fact that he never envisaged his work as a clean, aseptic kind of history, where one begins with a *tabula rasa* and carries on by providing neat structures on top. Foucault has not produced positivist histories of this kind. He was always interested in discourses that intersect, overlap and affect each other. Furthermore, unlike Derrida,

Foucault was to some extent a reluctant writer who preferred to work with a direct political agenda in which the effectiveness of the writing mattered, but the effectiveness of actions counted even more.

He was always interested in discourses that intersect, overlap and affect each other. Furthermore, unlike Derrida, Foucault was to some extent a reluctant writer who preferred to work with a direct political agenda in which the effectiveness of the writing mattered, but the effectiveness of actions counted even more.

Foucault's wish to keep his discourse clear made him communicate in a style that aimed to establish a meaningful dialogue and a platform for active engagement (Foucault 1986: 64). This is despite the fact that the space and the territory Foucault refers to are never stable and orderly, never Cartesian, but explorative, tilted and oblique, driven by experience and questions about perception and knowledge. What makes these unusual spaces special is the fact that Foucault's narratives provide sense to this complex geography, endowing it with the possibility for the next action or a fresh thought.

Foucault commented on the role of spatial concepts such as position, displacement, site, field, territory, domain, horizon, archipelago, region and landscape, with a brief genealogical summary of these terms' etymologies, pointing out that these words often had a military background. For example, consider the following: *displacement* is linked to the displacement of the army, a squadron or a population; *region* is derived from the military region (from *regere*, to command); and a *province* is a conquered territory (from pro-*vincere*). Foucault comments on other spatial terms such as *territory* and *domain* that are juridico-political notions and *field*, which is an economico-juridical term, while notions such as *horizon* and *landscape* are of pictorial provenance (Foucault 1986: 63–77, 68–9). Foucault showed the need for these notions in describing the relations between power and knowledge, and added that if knowledge were analysed in strategic terms (such as region, domain, implantation, displacement), then any further analyses of knowledge in respect to the relations of power would tend to unfold easily and 'transpire expressively' (Foucault 1986: 69).

## *On other spaces (heterotopia), history and heterogeneous space*

Foucault's intuition and eloquence in relation to space has attracted the attention of architects. His discussion on heterotopia is often mentioned in this context (see earlier discussion on cemeteries as heterotopia in Chapter 3). It is prefaced by an account of his 1966 participation at a workshop on space organised by a group of architects. The outcome of the discussion that took place in the Centre d'Étude d'Architecture in Paris was the text entitled 'On other spaces' (Foucault 1993). According to the prevailing interpretation of the event, a psychologist who took part in the workshop challenged Foucault for not thinking more dialectically – in terms of time.

Foucault often mentioned this episode to indicate the hegemony of the temporal paradigm over the spatial that was characteristic of the French (and wider) academic context prior to the 1960s. In this contest (*agon*) between space and time, Foucault deployed a method that took the form of discursive 'geography', which helped him to challenge the continuities of historiography and its period paradigms. Foucault thought that the modern pursuit of the question of origins has contributed to the understanding of the ontological significance of time. He challenged this significance and the examination led to the acknowledgement of space as a relevant intellectual category (Philo 1992: 141–3; West-Pavlov 2009: 112).

In this contest (*agon*) between space and time, Foucault

deployed a method that took the form of discursive

'geography', which helped him to challenge the continuities of historiography and its period paradigms. Foucault thought that the modern pursuit of the question of origins has contributed to the understanding of the ontological significance of time. He challenged this significance and the examination led to the acknowledgement of space as a relevant intellectual category.

Foucault argues that while the privileged category of the nineteenth century was history (and *time*) with its themes of development and stagnation, crises and cycles, the category that was gaining prominence in the late-twentieth century was that of *space*. According to Foucault, we are caught in the dialectic of this process. As he writes,

> We are in the age of the simultaneous, of juxtaposition, the near and the far, the side by side and the scattered. A period in which, in my view, the world is putting itself to test not so much as a great way of life destined to grow in time but as a net that links points together and creates its own muddle. It might be said that certain ideological conflicts, which underlie the controversies of our day take place between pious descendants of time and tenacious inhabitants of space (Foucault 1993: 420).

In the essay on heterotopia, Foucault outlined the history of Western space, which he says was hierarchical, comprising terrestrial places that were sacred and profane, urban and rural, protected or open and undefended (1993: 420). He highlights that according to cosmological theory, which was prevalent in the Middle Ages, super-celestial places existed in contrast to terrestrial places. Galileo opened up the 'medieval space', which Foucault called the space of localisation, when he asserted that space was infinite. In doing so, Foucault argued, Galileo dissolved the medieval space, which had a number of consequences including the understanding that the localisation of the thing was no longer fixed but had to be considered in the infinity of a cosmos that moved.

According to Foucault, this meant that rather than having something permanently fixed, we have temporary arrangements defined by relationships of proximity between elements, which in turn led to the problems of arrangements and position, demography and patterns of ordering. We read:

> In a still more concrete manner, the problem of position is posed for men in demographic terms. The question of the arrangement of the earth's inhabitants is not just one of knowing whether there will be enough room for all of them – a problem that is in any case of the greatest importance – but also one of knowing what are the relations of vicinity, what kind of storage, circulation, reference, and classification of human elements should take preference in this or that situation, according to the objective that is being sought. In our era, space represents itself to us in the form of patterns of ordering (Foucault 1993: 421).

While recalling the work of Bachelard, Foucault reminds us that we do not live in a homogeneous space, but in a space saturated with qualities: the space of our primary perception, of our dreams and of our passions, which holds intrinsic qualities – it can be light, ethereal, transparent, or dark, uneven, opaque, the space of heights and peaks or the space of mud and dungeons, flowing space or a stone-like fixed space. Foucault argues that the analyses of this kind, however fundamental, were primarily concerned with inner space. He, on the other hand, wished to speak of the external space, without locating the external space in opposition to the inner space, which he called a space of experience:

> The space in which we live, from which we are drawn out of ourselves, just where the erosion of our lives, our time, our history takes place, this space that wears us down and consumes us, is in itself heterogeneous. In other words we do not live in a sort of a vacuum... but in a set of relationships that define positions which cannot be equated or in any way superimposed (Foucault 1993: 421).

He, on the other hand, wished to speak of the external space, without locating the external space in opposition to the inner space, which he called a space of experience: 'The space in which we live, from which we are drawn out of ourselves, just where the erosion of our lives, our time, our history takes place, this space that wears us down and consumes us, is in itself heterogeneous.'

Foucault's particular interest is in the arrangement of spaces, which are endowed with the curious property of being in relation with all the others but in such a way as to 'suspend, neutralise, or invert' the set of relationships designed, reflected, or mirrored by themselves. These spaces, according to Foucault, are of two general types: utopias and heterotopias (Foucault 1993: 421–2). *Utopias* have no real space, but have a general relationship of direct or inverse analogy with the real space of society. These spaces are essentially unreal. *Heterotopias* on the other hand are real and effective spaces which are outlined in the very institution of society. Foucault writes,

> Heterotopias constitute a sort of counter-arrangement of effectively realised utopia, in which all the *real arrangements* ... that can be found within society, are at one and the same time *represented, challenged,* and *overturned*: a sort of place that lies *outside* all places and yet is actually *localisable* (Foucault 1993: 422).

Heterotopias are privileged, sacred or forbidden places, often reserved for the individual in a crisis. As such, heterotopia has the power of juxtaposing in a single real place different spaces and locations that are incompatible with each other, as in theatres and cinemas but also as in the traditional garden. Significantly, these spaces could be linked to different parts of time as in museums, libraries, fair grounds, holiday villages and so on (Foucault 1993: 419–36).

## Heterotopias are privileged, sacred or forbidden places, often reserved for the individual in a crisis.

Heterotopias have boundaries and a system of opening and closing that isolates them and makes them penetrable. Usually, one does not get into heterotopian location by one's own will; the person is either forced, as in the case of the barracks or the prison, or must submit to the rites of purification, as in ritual bathing and the like.

In Foucault's work, heterotopias seem to have a function that takes place between two opposite poles: on the one hand, they perform the task of creating a space of illusion that shows how the nature of 'real' space is more illusory; on the other, they have the function of forming another space, perfect and well-arranged, from which the present space emerges as disorderly.

It is important to observe that this 1967 essay on heterotopia that addressed the spaces of boarding schools and camps acted as a prologue that brought into analysis the spaces of prisons and barracks, which emerged as a major subject in *Discipline and Punish* seven years later. The next section outlines how the process of spatialisation of discourse happened.

### *Spatialisation of discourses: from spatial metaphor to discourse on space*

Figures that show the instances of discursive spatialisation in Foucault's writings include spatial comparisons, metaphors, configurations and strong lively images. They all have narrative, rhetorical and epistemological function and in various ways they assist the reader in conceiving complex thought.

Foucault distinguished the spatial metaphors used simply as description from the ones he 'advanced' and studied as objects. The latter he identified as those of the seventeenth century that showed the signs of epistemological transformations observable in the spatialisation of knowledge, which were the key factors in the constitution of knowledge as science (1991b: 254).

Significantly, this differentiation between the spatial metaphors as narratives and those Foucault studied and 'advanced' refers to their different usage, which discloses their gradual shift that made the *spatial metaphors mutate into the concepts of space*. This change is not insignificant for architects, as these concepts delineate a particular kind of space – Foucault's discursive space, or the space of discursive formation, where discourses interact with actual physical space in its institutional, architectural and urban form, for example in exhibitions, museums and similar (see Chapter 2, 'Statements, events, discursive formations'). This in turn opens new avenues of thought, as observed by Paul Veyne (1979), West-Pavlov (2009) and Paul Hirst (2005).

Paul Veyne, a historian and a close friend of Michel Foucault, was the first to point out this modification in Foucault's thinking (Veyne 1979: 203). Veyne and West-Pavlov, who quotes him, suggest that Foucault's thought moved from spatial discourse understood through its images and metaphors (*The Order of Things* and *The Archaeology of Knowledge*) into the realm of the actual space where discourse and architecture are part of the power relations and processes (*The Birth of the Clinic* and *Discipline and Punish*).

Veyne and West-Pavlov, who quotes him, suggest that Foucault's thought moved from spatial discourse understood through its images and metaphors (*The Order of Things and The Archaeology of Knowledge*) into the realm of the actual space where discourse and architecture are part of the power relations and processes (*The Birth of the Clinic* and *Discipline and Punish*).

Foucault has repeatedly argued that the ultimate structural reason for his thought being spatial was in the fact that the spatial metaphors he used depended upon the classical knowledge of the seventeenth and eighteenth century that was constituted through the spatialisation of objects of science. Already present in the natural history as classified by Linnaeus, the rule of analysis was to study only that which was visible in the object that was spatialised. Consequently, Foucault maintains, this condition had to re-emerge in the analysis (1991b: 254). He explains,

> **What is striking about the epistemological mutations and transformations that occurred in the seventeenth century is the way the spatialisation of knowledge made up one of the factors allowing the elaboration of this knowledge to produce science. If Linnaeus' natural history and classifications were possible, it was for the certain number of reasons…. The object was spatialised (Foucault 1994: 283–4; West-Pavlov 2009: 115).**

Already present in the natural history as classified by Linnaeus, the rule of analysis was to study only that which was visible in the object that was spatialised. Consequently, Foucault maintains, this condition had to re-emerge in the analysis.

Foucault recognised that this spatial distribution of the objects of knowledge occurred according to principles of the structure such as the number of elements, their arrangement and their width and height. There were also other instances of spatial distribution and media which contributed to the production of knowledge through the deployment of different techniques such as illustration, printing and bookmaking. These techniques acted as particular mechanisms that framed the content, which was on the way to becoming recognised as part of scientific knowledge.

There were also other instances of spatial distribution and

media which contributed to the production of knowledge

through the deployment of different techniques such as

illustration, printing and bookmaking. These techniques acted

as particular mechanisms that framed the content, which

was on the way to becoming recognised as part of scientific

knowledge.

Thus the manner of representation, its spacing and its framing of the object have direct effects upon any possible knowledge about the object. In this context, both architecture and its drawings, its models and its other spatial, experiential instances all have an impact upon concepts, knowledge and practice. While Foucault specifically demonstrates how this has worked for scientific discourse, the same episteme underlies architecture and the related arts.

For example, within the seventeenth century context of London and England, polymaths such as Robert Hooke and Christopher Wren used the work of the graphic artist and etcher Wenceslaus Hollar (1607–77) in the conduct of their scientific experiments as well as in proposing their architectural and urban design projects (Fontana-Giusti 2012: 21–33). Hollar's topographical representations of the city of London were considered the best evidence of the city's urban configuration. In his diaries, Hooke stated that they were executed by a 'scientific method' applied by Hollar to his 'encyclopaedic investigation of nature and human history'. Having accurately denoted the buildings and their plots of land, before and after the Great Fire of London, these representations were subsequently used as legally binding scientific documents for the rebuilding of London and its major buildings, including St Paul's Cathedral. In this way, Hollar's representations with their spatial versatility and limitations determined the field of architectural knowledge and practice that followed (Fontana-Giusti 2012: 21–33).

Foucault concludes that the seventeenth-century mutation of knowledge was an important stage of epistemic conversion in the classical period as the spatial techniques were not simply metaphors, but actions (Foucault 1991b: 254). The specified spatiality of objects and organisms established during the classical period provided the basic grid that made possible further 'framings' of the objects of scientific studies in the production of knowledge. Because Foucault excavates and observes the aspects of this spatiality and their effects on knowledge in most of his works, he manages to unearth and disclose the spaces into which objects, statements and knowledge were set, positioned and spatialised in order to become concepts.

Foucault concludes that the seventeenth-century mutation of knowledge was an important stage of epistemic conversion in the classical period as the spatial techniques were not simply metaphors, but actions.

## 5.2 Avant-garde and the language of space

In elaborating innovatively on the spatiality of concepts, statements and knowledge, Foucault relied on the works of the avant-garde artists and thinkers. Like Nietzsche, Foucault privileges the non-traditional subjects of philosophy such as literature, art and music as liminal domains of life where the new episteme first shows up. This approach is evident in Foucault's interest and exploration of the twentieth-century avant-garde writings of Raymond Roussel (2004), Georges Bataille (1977) and Maurice Blanchot (1989). We shall now briefly address this domain of Foucault's work centring on *Death and the Labyrinth* (2004) and related essays.

The discovery of radical notions such as the 'transgression', investigated by Bataille, and 'literary space' (*espace littéraire*), conceived initially by Blanchot, was important for Foucault (2001: 205–15; 1998: 21–32; Philo 1992: 144–8), who maintained that in these works we can observe how twentieth-century conditions were breaking away from previous practices of art and language, thus bringing them into a different realm – that of space:

> The 20th century is perhaps the era in which such kinships were undone. … This … reveals that language is or, perhaps became a thing of space. … And if space is in today's language, the most obsessive of metaphors, it is not that it henceforth offers the only recourse; *but it is in space that, from the outset, language unfurls, slips on itself, determines its choices, draws its figures and translations. It is in space… that its very being 'metaphorizes' itself.* The gap, distance, the intermediary, dispersion, fracture and difference are not the themes of literature today, but that in which language is now given and comes to us: what makes it speak (2001: 163–4; West-Pavlov 2009: 117, emphasis mine).

Aspects of this discourse on active and heterogeneous space appear in Foucault's exploration of the world of Raymond Roussel, with whom he seems to have identified. He was captivated with Roussel the man – as dandy, aesthete, obsessional, depressive, Romantic, experimentalist, homosexual and *enfant terrible* of French bourgeoisie (2004: xiii). Foucault credits Roussel for sharing the same cosmos as the themes they had in common remained tangible throughout Foucault's work (e.g. the spatial functioning of the system of language, experimentations in textuality and the disbelief in the myth of origins).

He was captivated with Roussel the man – as dandy,

aesthete, obsessional, depressive, Romantic, experimentalist,

homosexual and *enfant terrible* of French bourgeoisie.

Foucault credits Roussel for sharing the same cosmos as the themes they had in common remained tangible throughout Foucault's work (e.g. the spatial functioning of the system of language, experimentations in textuality and the disbelief in the myth of origins).

In *Death and the Labyrinth*, Foucault seems to dissolve into Roussel, as we can read the book in conjunction with two other related essays written at the same time: 'So Cruel a Knowledge' (1962) and 'Language and Infinity' (1963) (Foucault 1998: 89–102 and 53–69). Saturated with Rousselian imagery such as the cascades of mirrors, labyrinths, minotaurs and other grotesques machines, the former essay comments on the late-eighteenth-century romances, while the latter addresses language and its metamorphosis, closing with the observation that the space of transformation from the natural into counternatural is the space of the transgressive (1998: 68). Both essays focus on language where 'words are in pursuit of objects' but where 'language constantly crashes down'. Foucault describes this as 'A work of language is the body of language crossed by death in order to open this infinite space where doubles reverberate' (Foucault 1998: 93). The same idea of reverberating doubles reappears in *Death and the Labyrinth*:

> There, between what is hidden within the evident and what is luminous in the inaccessible, the task of language is found. It's easy to understand why André Breton and others after him have seen in Roussel's work an obsession with the hidden, the invisible, and the withheld. ... Roussel's language shows that the visible and the not visible repeat each other infinitely, and this duplication of the same gives language its significance (Foucault 2004: 122–3).

Saturated with Rousselian imagery such as the cascades of mirrors, labyrinths, minotaurs and other grotesques machines, the former essay comments on the late-eighteenth-century romances, while the latter addresses language and its metamorphosis, closing with the observation that the space of transformation from the natural into counternatural is the space of the transgressive. Both essays focus on language where 'words are in pursuit of objects' but where 'language constantly crashes down'. Foucault describes this as 'A work of language is the body of language crossed by death in order to open this infinite space where doubles reverberate'.

Foucault states that it is not that language wants to conceal anything; language simply exists as that hidden duplicate of the visible. He maintains that this is the function that language has from the moment it begins to flow among concrete objects and it is the reason why things are perceptible only through language. He writes,

> But this sweet shadow which beneath the surface and the mask makes things visible and describable, isn't it from the moment of birth, the proximity of death, that death which reduplicates the world like peeling the fruit (2004: 123).

We could emphasise again that for Foucault (and many thinkers of his generation), language was a major issue and a foremost focus of studies. Language was no longer simply transmitting content from the past to the present. In Foucault's words 'language gave up its uninterrupted re-presentation of a meaning' and became *spaced-out* – spread over distance, dispersed and broken-up. Foucault thus recognised the condition of language as autonomous from the system of rationality as established during the eighteenth and nineteenth century.

Language was no longer simply transmitting content from the past to the present. In Foucault's words 'language gave up its uninterrupted re-presentation of a meaning' and became *spaced-out* – spread over distance, dispersed and broken-up. Foucault thus recognised the condition of language as autonomous from the system of rationality as established during the eighteenth and nineteenth century.

### *The curve and the spiral of rationality*

Foucault argued that this spacing-out of language is at work in avant-garde literature, where the language *delinearised* itself. Here, the language of classical narrative literature opened itself up laterally – transversally. Thus, literature became the place where language stopped 'orderly representing meaning' in usual linear fashion and began 'semiotizing', i.e. 'going off the beaten track' into a transversal mode and experimentation (West-Pavlov 2009: 117–8).

Foucault has addressed this dispersion of language by contrasting the traditional nineteenth-century type of literature and its straight plot 'line', with the paradoxical 'curve' of a graph:

> This paradoxical 'curve', so different from the Homeric return or from the
> fulfilment of the Promise, is without doubt for the moment the unthinkable of
> literature. Which is to say that which makes it possible (Foucault 2007: 164).

The literary works by Guillaume Apollinaire, James Joyce and Vladimir
Mayakovsky played a role in the modernist project that questioned the
conditions of writing, which greatly appealed to Foucault. The French
philosopher extracted and formulated their lessons philosophically and spatially.
In the words of another French thinker and revolutionary psychoanalyst,
Felix Guattari, these projects led to the discourse that managed to escape
linear structure and assume transversality, and the paradoxical curving of yet
unthinkable space that opened up (Guattari 1972).

It could be concluded that Foucault had thus used avant-garde examples to
draw our attention to the detail that space had remained the un-thought
within traditional literature. By following the thread of the avant-garde writers
and being affected by their work, which converted the linearity of the text into
different aspects of space and language, Foucault demonstrated the underlying
conditions of thought and language.

Texts such as *The Order of Things* drew from this awareness, which subjected
Foucault's own language to the dynamism of change. The trajectory of this
change went from allusions in the space of literature to carefully constructed
concepts in his more epistemologically aware works. His language does not let
our thought remain inert within its secure mode for long, as the figures of this
language constantly push our thoughts further.

The figure of a curve and its extended three-dimensional form – a spiral –
appeared in Foucault's 1982 interview with Paul Rabinow in relation to the
question of postmodernism and rationality. Foucault was in agreement with
Habermas regarding the problem of rationality: if one abandons the works
of the philosophy of rationality, one runs a risk of falling into irrationality, he
argued. Throughout the 1980s it was important to maintain this position,
because of the perception that some post-structuralist philosophers (and even

more so their followers) embraced irrationality. Foucault admits that for him, the central issue in philosophy since the eighteenth century has always been, what is this Reason that we use? What are its effects, limits and its dangers? And above all how can we exist as rational beings, committed to practising a rationality that is simultaneously subject to intrinsic dangers? (Foucault 1991b: 249) He concludes that it is dangerous to identify Reason as the enemy that needs to be removed, while it is equally dangerous to say that critical questioning of rationality risks turning us to irrationality. The example he gives for this ambiguity is the fact that it was…

> …on the basis of flamboyant rationality of social Darwinism that racism was formulated, becoming one of the most enduring and powerful ingredients of Nazism. This was of course an irrationality, but an irrationality that was at the same time, after all, a certain form of rationality… (Foucault 1991b: 249).

Foucault admits that for him, the central issue in philosophy since the eighteenth century has always been, what is this Reason that we use? What are its effects, limits and its dangers? And above all how can we exist as rational beings, committed to practising a rationality that is simultaneously subject to intrinsic dangers?

The complex situation that Foucault describes is of vital importance, because if philosophy is to have a critical function, then it should be within the domain where it would be able

> to accept this sort of spiral, this sort of revolving door of rationality that refers us to its necessity, to its indispensability and, at the same time, to its intrinsic dangers (Foucault 1991b: 249).

What started as a discussion on a paradoxical curve in Foucault's work in relation to language becomes a three-dimensional configuration in the form of a spiral of rationality, where the figure of the spiral is not simply a metaphor but a clear model – the extension of Foucault's discourse in the sense of the logical conclusion of his arguments.

What started as a discussion on a paradoxical curve in Foucault's work in relation to language becomes a three-dimensional configuration in the form of a spiral of rationality, where the figure of the spiral is not simply a metaphor but a clear model – the extension of Foucault's discourse in the sense of the logical conclusion of his arguments.

It is thus possible to construe that for Foucault, space and language live in this close symbiotic partnership, where any modifications are mutually effective, where any alterations to space will inflict consequences upon language, while the mutation in language will always make a move and affect space. Indeed, where space and language cohabit, architecture cannot be far away. This is why architecture is the unspoken constant in Foucault's work.

## 5.3 Deleuzian century

### Reversing Platonism, phantasm and topology

Despite the fact that from the 1990s onwards, architectural theory entered the new territory with a number of paradigms such as the fold, biomorphism or parametricism, Foucault's discourse on space has remained invaluable and original. Indeed, many of these developments could be traced back to the legacy of Foucault's radical approach. It came down to Gilles Deleuze and Felix

Guattari to publish a critical discourse that radically addressed spatiality (1987: 474–500). As foreseen by Foucault in 1970, Deleuze's (and Guattari's) work has resonated strongly with all those concerned with space.

In 'Theatrum Philosophicum', a critical essay on *Difference and Repetition* and *The Logic of Sense*, Foucault discusses Deleuze's ideas, a process during which his language, space and concepts constantly challenge each other (Foucault 1977: 165–96). The discussion that takes us through the history of thought and that shows Foucault's understating of Deleuze's intuitive discourse is introduced as follows:

> I must discuss two books of exceptional merit and importance: *Difference and Repetition* and *The Logic of Sense*. Indeed, these books are so outstanding that they are difficult to discuss; this may explain, as well, why so few have undertaken this task. I believe that these works will continue to revolve about us in enigmatic resonance with those of Klossowski, another major excessive sign, and perhaps one day this century will be known as Deleuzian (Foucault 1977: 165).

It could be argued today that the Deleuzian epoch has arrived, exemplified in the extravagant architecture of the Bilbao Guggenheim museum, the scaled-up organic geometry of the Beijing Olympic stadium, the futuristic spatial eccentricities of The Phaeno interactive science centre in Wolfsburg, and other innovative projects that appear to have endorsed Deleuzian, non-Platonic geometries and spaces. These buildings, known as either 'parametric' or as 'folds' belonging to the practice of 'folding', are not rectangular, flat, Cartesian or in any way subservient to the forms of Euclidean geometry. They either borrow their form from natural organisms or they develop it from chosen parameters whose function is reportedly expressed in the agreed formula, which will be applied spatially, resulting in a form that, due to the complexity of the processes, only computers can develop. These buildings are significantly different from those built at the time when Foucault questioned the dominancy of traditional forms such as the circle or sphere and when, acknowledging the ambition that aimed to overturn the Platonic forms, he wrote:

The circle must be abandoned as a faulty principle of return; we must abandon our tendency to organise everything into a sphere. All things return into straight and narrow, by way of a straight and labyrinthine line. Thus, fibrils and bifurcations (Leiris' marvellous series would be well suited to a Deleuzian analysis) (Foucault 1977: 166).

It could be argued today that the Deleuzian epoch has arrived, exemplified in the extravagant architecture of the Bilbao Guggenheim museum, the scaled-up organic geometry of Beijing Olympic stadium, the futuristic spatial eccentricities of The Phaeno interactive science centre in Wolfsburg, and other innovative projects that appear to have endorsed Deleuzian, non-Platonic geometries and spaces.

On one level, Foucault clearly forecast the architecture of the fold, fibrils and bifurcations as the future of architecture. On the other, it remains to be seen what else has been suggested in this juxtaposition of Deleuze and Platonism. As Foucault's and Deleuze's texts open up more levels for architectural projection and analyses, they also allow for more innovative possibilities for architecture to appear in the future. This therefore goes beyond the current production into yet unattained areas of work. While the cynics' claims about the convenient correspondence between the curvy parametric buildings of recent times and rhetorical authority of Deleuze and Guattari might be appropriate, it does not disqualify Foucault's predictions about Deleuzian space.

On one level, Foucault clearly forecast the architecture of the fold, fibrils and bifurcations as the future of architecture. On the other, it remains to be seen what else has been suggested in this juxtaposition of Deleuze and Platonism.

### What are the further implications?

It is possible that Foucault was aiming to question and exceed the 'systems of thought' by pushing the boundaries of their intelligibility. He did so primarily by suggesting that Platonism has a counterpoint – the geometry of phantasms and intangible objects. As Foucault suggests, to reverse Platonism with Deleuze 'is to displace oneself insidiously within it, to descend a notch, to descend to its smallest gestures – discrete, but *moral* – which serve to exclude the simulacrum' (Foucault 1977: 167).

It is possible that Foucault was aiming to question and exceed the 'systems of thought' by pushing the boundaries of their intelligibility. He did so primarily by suggesting that Platonism has a counterpoint – the geometry of phantasms and intangible objects. As Foucault suggests, to reverse Platonism with Deleuze 'is to displace oneself insidiously within it, to descend a notch, to descend to its smallest gestures – discrete, but *moral* – which serve to exclude the simulacrum'.

In this way, Foucault argues for a way of thinking about space which goes beyond the established worn-out system of representations (simulacra), which is imitative and therefore not truthful, open or imaginative. Within this trajectory, he calls for small and discrete gestures that would gradually bridge the gap between geometry and phantasm. Because these gestures call for the revision of the existing limitations and inadequacies in our conception of space, which have determined and penetrated almost all domains of knowledge and structures of society, Foucault sees this pursuit as emancipatory and hence 'moral'. Some parametric architectural projects have worked within these premises and have stated their aspirations along these lines, although the results are more difficult to acknowledge (Schumacher 2010).

Excluding simulacra is a major problem for Western culture, as it is difficult to exclude that structure which is in the very fabric of the culture built upon representation. Yet there is a moral argument for its possible exclusion. In this respect, Foucault points towards the surfaces and the emergence of phantasm – the intangible object. He suggests the possibility of integration of these objects into our thought. He calls for the articulation of a philosophy of the phantasm that cannot be reduced to a 'fact' through the intermediary of perception or of an image, in a way in which we think of concepts as images (in the manner of Locke). This, according to Foucault, cannot be pursued, as a fixed image is clearly not phantasm's logical domain. He recalls the phantasm which

> arises between surfaces, where it assumes meaning, and in the reversal that causes every interior to pass to the outside and every exterior to the inside, in the temporal oscillation that always makes it precede and follow itself – in short, in what Deleuze would perhaps not allow us to call its 'incorporeal materiality' (Foucault 1977: 169).

Excluding simulacra is a major problem for Western culture, as it is difficult to exclude that structure which is in the very fabric of the culture built upon representation. Yet there is a moral argument for its possible exclusion. In this respect,

Foucault points towards the surfaces and the emergence of phantasm – the intangible object. He suggests the possibility of integration of these objects into our thought. He calls for the articulation of a philosophy of the phantasm that cannot be reduced to a 'fact' through the intermediary of perception or of an image, in a way in which we think of concepts as images (in the manner of Locke).

Foucault recognises that it is useless to search for a more substantial truth behind the phantasm or to reduce it to an image or another intermediary of perception. Phantasms need to be accepted for what they are: in their essence they have

> to function at the limit of the bodies; against the bodies, because they stick to bodies and protrude from them, but also because they touch them, cut them, break them into sections, regionalize them, and multiply their surfaces; and equally, outside the bodies, because they function between bodies according to laws of proximity, torsion and variable distance – laws of which they remain ignorant. Phantasms do not extend organisms into an imaginary domain; they topologize the materiality of the body (1977: 169–70).

Phantasms need to be accepted for what they are: in their essence they have 'to function at the limit of the bodies; against the bodies, because they stick to bodies and protrude from them, but also because they touch them, cut them, break them into sections, regionalize them, and multiply their surfaces'.

Phantasms do not extend organisms into an imaginary domain; they topologize the materiality of the body.

Topology (concerned with properties of space such as connectedness, based on continuous deformation, bending and stretching) thus becomes a new ground for all. Foucault argues that Deleuze's *Logique du sens* can be read as the most alien book imaginable from the point of view of phenomenologist Merleau-Ponty (1908–61, a French philosopher who emphasised the importance of perception and built his ideas upon the works of Marx, Husserl and Heidegger). Controversially for his time, Foucault continues,

> ... according to Deleuze, phantasms form the impenetrable and incorporeal surface of bodies; and from this process, simultaneously topological and cruel, something is shaped that falsely presents itself as a centered organism and that distributes at its periphery the increasing remoteness of things (Foucault 1977: 170).

From today's perspective, it is easy to underestimate the significance of Foucault's early endorsement of Deleuze's work in 1970. This wholehearted, generous intellectual grasp of his colleague's extraordinary opus, which Foucault saw as 'the boldest and the most insolent of metaphysical treatises', was daring and risky but also strategically significant and emancipating for the overall course of critical thinking.

### Theatre, events and the new archivist

In order to expand further this discourse on phantasm and simulacrum as articulated in the first part of 'Theatrum Philosophicum', Foucault introduces the discussion about psychoanalysis and the theatre. He writes about these

two privileged stages of life describing their status within the conditions
and dynamism of liberated simulacra. He argues that psychoanalysis should
eventually be understood as a metaphysical practice, since it concerns itself
with phantasms, and that the theatre is a special polyscenic place,

> **... where we encounter, without any trace of representation (copying or
> imitating), the dance of masks, the cries of bodies, and the gesturing of
> hands and fingers (Foucault 1977: 171).**

Foucault concludes that it is impossible to reconcile these two series and thus
to reduce them to either perspective, as Freud, psychoanalyst and physician,
and Artaud, dramatist, poet and actor, exclude each other (1977: 172).
Moreover, both psychoanalysis and the theatre consist and unfold into *events* –
the elementary category in the formation of discourses.

In this essay, the movement of Foucault's thought constantly escalates from the
spaces of Plato to those of the Sophists, the Cynics and Epicurus, casting up
his reflections with irony and humour. He reconstructs a genealogical system of
ancient philosophies (Foucault 1977: 168–9) by taking us through the labyrinth
of thoughts which are, according to Foucault, 'at the level of their existence –
perilous acts'. We thus reach 'theatrum philosophicum' – philosophy as theatre,
which is how Foucault describes Deleuze's thought. Deleuzian thinking, as
understood by Foucault, does not lie in the future, but is present and lively
in his texts 'springing forth, dancing before us, in our midst; genital thought,
intensive thought, affirmative thought, acategorical thought' (1977: 196).

We thus reach 'theatrum philosophicum' – the philosophy as
theatre, which is how Foucault describes Deleuze's thought.
Deleuzian thinking, as understood by Foucault, does not lie in
the future, but is present and lively in his texts 'springing forth,

dancing before us, in our midst; genital thought, intensive thought, affirmative thought, acategorical thought'.

Foucault admits that in this theatre, he first sees each of the ideas as unrecognisable faces – as masks not seen before. Nevertheless, they become identifiable as they are the masks of Plato, Duns Scotus, Spinoza, Leibniz, Kant and all the other philosophers that appear in Deleuze's work and whom Foucault recalls while telling us that the philosophy approached in this Deleuzian way is no longer a thought but a theatre:

> **This is a theatre where the explosive laughter of Sophists tears through the mask of Socrates; where Spinoza's methods conduct a wild dance in a decentered circle while substance revolves about it like a mad planet (1977: 196).**

In pursuing the scope and the logic of this thinking, Foucault establishes different explanations for a number of concepts, including those of the theatre and the archive. For this reason, Deleuze subsequently called Foucault 'the new archivist' (Deleuze 2006: 3–21) – the record-keeper, who sees this space not as the sum total of events and things that have been recorded but as the *system that governs what can be recorded*. (On Foucault and archives, see Chapter 2 of this book.)

In this sense, the archives are not the census, the notebooks, sketchbooks, antiquarian documents or recovered works of architecture, but the series of events and mentalities that made any listing possible. By reiterating Deleuze's approach from yet another angle, Foucault implicitly argues that his method is not the science of collecting and recovering material things but something like a theatre – the never completed, never wholly achieved project.

While the pleasure of Deleuzian space and time might appear tempting, there is a limit, as uncritical playfulness becomes not pleasure but pain. The instance of the limits of spatial

*jouissance* in reading Deleuze is identified by Douglas Spencer.

While the pleasure of Deleuzian space and time might appear tempting, there is a limit, as uncritical playfulness becomes not pleasure but pain. The instance of the limits of spatial *jouissance* in reading Deleuze is identified by Douglas Spencer. On the related matter of architectural reading of Deleuze's work, Spencer argues that 'Deleuzism' in architecture has tended to read the philosophy of Deleuze and Guattari with a marked bias particularly against Marxian register (2011: 9–21). Spencer rightly outlines that in this way, architects have by and large disregarded socio-political aspects of Deleuze's and Guattari's work, something that Foucault never failed to recognise and argue for. In that sense, Spencer refers to Foreign Office Architects (FOA) and Alessandro Zaera Polo, who initially extracted from the work of Deleuze and Guattari a number of concepts that appeared to lend themselves readily to translation into spatial concepts. Significantly, Spencer argues, Zaera Polo has more recently returned to the question of the political, previously announced as ephemeral to the concerns of architecture (Zaera Polo and Moussavi 2003: 10), aligning his interpretation closer to Foucault's reading of Deleuze and Guattari.

In that sense, Spencer refers to Foreign Office Architects (FOA)

and Alessandro Zaera Polo, who initially extracted from the

work of Deleuze and Guattari a number of concepts that

appeared to lend themselves readily to translation into spatial

concepts. Significantly, Spencer argues, Zaera Polo has more

recently returned to the question of the political, previously

announced as ephemeral to the concerns of architecture,

## aligning his interpretation closer to Foucault's reading of Deleuze and Guattari.

It could be argued that in a manner of going back to space as discussed by Foucault, Zaera Polo has acknowledged the need for acting politically by rethinking spatially the building envelope as the organisational and representational medium through which it contributes to social discipline and politics. In this way we can observe the continued relevance of Foucault's thought in relation to contemporary phenomena.

### 5.4 Ad finem

This last chapter has discussed the spatiality involved in Foucault's thinking by making it the subject of observation and theoretical scrutiny. It has shed light on how Foucault's spatial metaphors and space-related thinking, which emerged and thrived in his early texts, were pivotal for his later discourse on space in *The Order of Things*, *The Archaeology of Knowledge* and *Discipline and Punish*.

It is the specific nature of these two different usages of space and spatial thought that I aimed to highlight. They correspond to Foucault's two streams of critique: the first that breaks the conventions, investigates and founds new concepts; and the second that tests and explores the potential of these new concepts and paradigms by putting them in use.

In the later stages of his life, Foucault recognised this duality and its dynamism. This recognition provided him with a platform from which to reflect on his own work, as can be read in his autobiographical essay (Foucault 1998: 459–65).

This was touched upon in the introduction of this book, later referred to in the section on the analytic of finitude (in Chapter 4 see the section: Crisis, self and finitude) and returned to in this concluding chapter.

Foucault acknowledged that it was the connection of desire to reality (and not its withdrawal into forms of representation) that possessed revolutionary force. In that sense, his own desire was linked to the reality of the avant-garde, be it art and literature or social standing. This is why the avant-garde works remained important. Their involvement triggered and pushed Foucault's thought outside the assumed space of language and let it spread beyond the canon of philosophy and human sciences, thus creating a new heterogeneous space for contemplation and analysis. Foucault cherished this freedom of investigation and pursued it without abandoning the logic of rationality and a critical attitude based on systematic and methodological practice of doubt.

Foucault acknowledged that it was the connection of desire to reality (and not its withdrawal into forms of representation) that possessed revolutionary force. In that sense, his own desire was linked to the reality of the avant-garde, be it art and literature or social standing. This is why the avant-garde works remained important.

In this sense, Foucault's overall approach and his aesthetic pursuits coincide with each other in their constant dedication to theorising new experiences, their conditions and their effects. In other words, Foucault investigates the conditions of 'aesthesis' ('feeling', 'experience' or 'felt experience'), rather than the formal properties of objects including buildings. Through theorising new experiences and their spaces, he is interested in disclosing the order of the strange flux of life in which humans, words and things (including architecture) appear to themselves and to others.

In this sense, Foucault's overall approach and his aesthetic

pursuits coincide with each other in their constant dedication to

theorising new experiences, their conditions and their effects.

Foucault therefore systematically confronts the prevailing suppositions about what the human is, suppositions which have, contrary to their claims, imprisoned us. His works have shown the mechanisms of this phenomenon, suggesting that we need further clarity about what a person is and articulations about the capacity of humans to transcend what appears as natural.

The pleasure of knowing and understanding the world is vital for Foucault, which is why his work consists of untiring testing and explorations of the new concepts and spaces. He gives a telling definition of a work as,

> That which is susceptible of introducing a significant difference in the field of knowledge, at the cost of a certain difficulty for the author and the reader, with, however, the eventual recompense of a certain pleasure, that is to say of access to another figure of truth (Foucault 1998: ix).

This characterisation of work indicates the nature of the premise that underpins the works of science as well as the works of art and architecture. One gains knowledge at the cost of certain difficulty and this route of difficult experience is the route of problematisation leading to truth. It is in the nature of human thought to operate through encountering, experiencing and defining problems. Thought is 'what allows for a step back' from the usual manner of doing and reacting to things; it allows for putting itself forward as a thought-object (Foucault 1994: xxxviii). Whether in science, art or architecture, thought understood and lived in this way is always experienced as liberty.

One gains knowledge at the cost of certain difficulty and this

route of difficult experience is the route of problematisation leading to truth. It is in the nature of human thought to operate

through encountering, experiencing and defining problems.

Thought is 'what allows for a step back' from the usual

manner of doing and reacting to things; it allows for putting

itself forward as a thought-object. Whether in science, art or

architecture, thought understood and lived in this way is always

experienced as liberty.

Throughout his work, life and travels, Foucault implied that it is impossible
to live well without living prudently, courageously and temperately, without
having relationships, and without caring for the other. This implies a certain
conviction that there is in the other something demanding of respect.
We appear and form ourselves in relation to the other and through our
problematisation of situations and events around us. Our personality emerges
in the intersection of the relations that are formed in this way. In this mutuality
of exchange, we discover what 'person' means and who we are, including who
we are as architects.

In that sense, Michel Foucault could be seen as a relational, conversational
philosopher whose work is a form of environment-building activity for his
readers. The effects of this environment and its spatiality are evident in the
work that continues to emerge.

Foucault several weeks before his death in the garden of the Musée Rodin, Paris. May 1984.

# Further reading...

There are numerous architectural historians and theorists whose work is closely or indirectly related to Foucault's. To recall them all is impossible; in addition to those already mentioned, we need to include a selected few.

Gilles Deleuze's book *Foucault* (1996) touches upon a number of issues proposed in both the 'Theatrum Philosophicum' and *The Archaeology of Knowledge* (Deleuze: 2006), while Deleuze and Guattari's *Thousand Plateaus* (1988) is the logical further reading.

Many of John Rajchman's writings, including *Michel Foucault: The Freedom of Philosophy* (1985) and 'Foucault's Art of Seeing' (*October*, 1988), are important contributions to the continuous dialogue with Foucault.

Christine Boyer, in her work on *The City and Collective Memory* (1996), investigates historical imagery and architectural entertainment by making multiple references to Foucault and his spatiality.

Mark Cousins's and Athar Houssain's *Michel Foucault* (1984) is a valuable intellectual summary of the major arguments. Didier Eribon's biography of *Michel Foucault* (1993) remains the most reliable bibliographical source book, while David Macey's (2004) take on Michel Foucault offers interesting reading.

# Bibliography

*Main works by Michel Foucault*

*Books (in chronological order of their original publication in French with details of their English translations)*

Foucault, M. (1954) (1987) *Mental Illness and Psychology*, trans. A. Sheridan, forward by H. Dreyfus. Berkeley, Los Angeles and London: University of California Press.

—— (1961) (2009) *Madness and Civilisation: A History of Insanity in the Age of Reason*, trans. R. Howard. London and New York: Routledge Abridged version.

—— (1963) (2010) *The Birth of the Clinic: An Archaeology of Medical Perception*, trans. A. M. Sheridan-Smith. London and New York: Routledge.

—— (1963) (2004) *Death and the Labyrinth: The World of Raymond Roussel*, trans. C. Raus. London and New York: Continuum.

—— (1966) (1991) *The Order of Things: An Archaeology of the Human Sciences*, trans. A. M. Sheridan Smith. London and New York: Routledge.

—— (1968) (1982) *This is Not a Pipe*, trans. J. Harkness. Berkeley: University of California Press.

—— (1969) (1985) *The Archaeology of Knowledge,* trans. A. M. Sheridan Smith. London: Routledge.

—— (1975) (1991a) *Discipline and Punish: The Birth of the Prison*, trans. A. M. Sheridan Smith. London: Penguin Books.

—— (1976) (1987a) *The History of Sexuality, Vol. 1: An Introduction,* trans. R. Hurley. London: Penguin Books.

—— (1984) (1987b) *The History of Sexuality, Vol. 2: The Use of Pleasure*, trans. R. Hurley. London: Penguin Books.

—— (1984) (1990) *The History of Sexuality, Vol. 3: The Care of the Self*, trans. R. Hurley. London: Penguin Books.

*Editions originally compiled and published in English*

—— (1977) *Language, Counter-Memory, Practice: Selected Essays and Interviews*, D. F. Bouchard, ed. D. F. Bouchard, trans. S. Simon. Ithaca, NY: Cornell University Press.

—— (1986) *Power/Knowledge: Selected Interviews and Other Writings, 1972–1977*. C. Gordon, ed. Brighton: The Harvester Press.

—— (1991b) *The Foucault Reader*. Rabinow, P. ed. New York: Pantheon.

*Articles, collections and interviews*

—— (1952) (1985a) *Dream, Imagination, and Existence*, trans, F. Williams. Ludwig Binswanger, 'Dream and Existence', trans. J. Needleman, *Studies of Existential Psychology and Psychiatry*.

—— (1964) (2007) 'The Language of Space' trans. G. Moore in J. W. Crampton and S. Elden, (eds)., *Space, Knowledge and Power*. Aldershot: Ashgate, 163–8.

—— (1967) 'On other spaces' (1993) in Ockman, J. ed. *Architecture Culture 1943–68*. New York: Columbia Books of Architecture, 419–26.

—— (1984) *Revue de l'Université Bruxelles* 113: 1984: 35–46.

—— (1985a) 'La Vie: L'Expérience et la Science', *Revue de Métaphysique et de Morale* 1, 6–14.

—— (1989) *Résumés des cours (1970–82)*. Paris: Julliard.

—— (1994) *Dits et écrits 1954–88*, vol. 4. Paris: Gallimard.

—— 'Des Traveaux' (1994) in *Dits et écrits*. Paris: Gallimard, vol. 4.

—— (1998) *Aesthetics, Method, and Epistemology*. J. D. Faubion, ed., P. Rabinow, series ed. New York: The New Press, Essential Works of Foucault, 1945–1984, vol. 2.

—— (2001) *Dits et écrits: 1954–1975*, vol. 1. Paris: Gallimard.

*Other works by Michel Foucault*

—— (1966) 'Philosophy and the Death of God', originally an interview with M. G. Foy, published in *Connaissance des homes* 22 (Autumn 1966), Carrette J. ed. (1999).

—— (1968) 'History, Discourse and Discontinuity', trans. A. M. Nazzaro, in *Salmagundi* 20 (Summer-Fall 1972) 225–48. Originally published as 'Reponse à une question', Esprit 5.

—— (1971) 'A Conversation with M. Foucault', *Partisan Review* 2.

—— (1971) 'Orders of Discourse', trans. R. Swyer, in *Social Science Information*, 10:2, 7–30.

—— (1971) 'Monstrosities in Criticism' trans. R. J. Matthews, *diacritics.* 1 (Fall 1971) 57–60.

—— (1971) 'Foucault Responds/2', *diacritics* 1 (Winter 1971) 60.

—— (1974) 'Michel Foucault on Attica: An Interview', *Telos* 19, 154–61.

—— (1975) ed. *I, Pierre Riviere, having slaughtered my mother, my sister, and my brother ...: A Case of Paracide in the 19th Century*, trans. F. Jelinek, ed. M. Foucault. New York: Pantheon.

—— (1977) 'The Political Function of the Intellectual', trans. Colin Gordon. *Radical Philosophy* 17 (Summer 1977) 12–15.

—— (1977) 'Power and Sex' trans. D. J. Parent. *Telos* 32 (Summer 1977).

—— (1980) *Herculine Barbin; Being the Recently Discovered Memoirs of a Nineteenth-Century French Hermaphrodite,* trans. R. McDougall. New York: Pantheon Books.

—— (1981) 'The Order of Discourse', trans. I. McLeod, in *Untying the Text: A Post-Structuralist Reader.* R. Young, ed. Boston and London: Routledge, Kegan Paul. 51–78.

—— with Sennett R. (1981) 'Sexuality and Solitude', *London Review of Books* (21 May 1981) 3–7.

—— (1981) 'Is it Useful to Revolt?', *Philosophy and Social Criticism* 8.

—— (1981) *Remarks on Marx: Conversations with Duccio Trombadori*, trans. R. J. Goldstein and J. Cascaito. New York: Semiotext(e), 1991. Foreign Agents series.

—— (1982) 'Is it Really Important to Think?', *Philosophy and Social Criticism* 9 (Spring 1982).

—— (1982) 'Response to Susan Sontag', *Soho News* (2 March 1982) 13.

—— (1983) 'Structuralism and Post-structuralism: An Interview with Gerard Raulet', *Telos* 55 (Spring 1983) 195–211.

—— (1984) 'Qu'appelle-t-on punir? Entretien avec Michel Foucault', *Revue de l'Université Bruxelles* 113: 35–46.

—— (1985) 'Final Interview', *Raritan* 5 (Summer 1985).

—— (1986) 'Kant on Enlightenment and Revolution', trans. C. Gordon, in *Economy and Society* 15:1 (February 1986) 88–96.

—— (1987) 'The Ethic of Care for the Self as a Practice of Freedom: An Interview with Michel Foucault', *Philosophy and Social Criticism* 12 (Summer 1987).

[——] Florence, M. (1988) '(Auto)biography, Michel Foucault 1926–1984', *History of the Present 4*, Spring, 259–85.

—— (1988). *Technologies of the Self: A Seminar with Michel Foucault,* L. H. Martin, H. Gutman, and P. H. Hutton, (eds). Amherst, MA: University of Massachusetts Press.

—— (1989) *Foucault Live (Interviews, 1966–84),* trans. J. Johnston and S. Lotringer, ed. New York: Semiotext(e), Foreign Agents series.

—— (1993) 'About the Beginnings of the Hermeneutics of the Self: Two Lectures at Dartmouth', *Political Theory* 21 (May 1993) 198–227.

—— (1995) 'Madness, the Absence of Work', trans. P. Stastny and Deniz Sengel. *Critical Inquiry* 21 (Winter 1995) 290–8.

—— (1997) *The Politics of Truth,* Sylvere Lotringer and Lysa Hochroth, (eds). New York: Semiotext(e).

—— (1997) *Ethics: Subjectivity and Truth,* Paul Rabinow, ed. New York: The New Press.

—— (1999) 'Philosophy and the Death of God', originally an interview with M. G. Foy published in *Connaissance des homes*, no 22. Autumn 1966, Carrette J. ed.

—— (1999) *Foucault and the Environment,* E. Darier, ed. Oxford: Blackwell.

—— (2000) *Power.* C. Gordon, ed, P. Rabinow, series ed. New York: The New Press, 298–325.

—— (2005) *The Hermeneutics of the Subject: Lectures at the Collège de France 1981–1982.* New York and Basingstoke: Palgrave/Macmillan.

—— (2009) *Manet and the Object of Painting,* trans. M. Barr. London: Tate Publishing.

**Secondary sources**

Allen, S. (1997) 'From object to field', *AD Profile 127 Architecture after Geometry, Architectural Design* 67:5/6, 24–31.

Agrest, D., Conway, P. and Weisman L., (eds) (1996) *The Sex of Architecture.* New York: Harry N. Abrams.

Barkan, L. ( 1999) *Unearthing the Past: Archaeology and Aesthetics in the Making of Renaissance Culture.* New Haven and London: Yale University Press.

Bloomer, J. (1995) *Architecture and Text: The (S)crypts of Joyce and Piranesi.* New Haven and London: Yale University Press, 3–10.

—— (1993) *'... and venustas', AA Files* 25. London: Architectural Association.

Boyer, M. C. (1996) *The City of Collective Memory.* London and Cambridge, MA: The MIT Press.

Bruno, G. (2007) *Public Intimacy: Architecture and the Visual Arts.* Cambridge, MA and London: The MIT Press.

Butler, J. (1990) *Gender Trouble: Feminism and Subversion of Identity.* London and New York: Routledge.

Carrette, J., ed. (1999) *Religion and Culture by Michel Foucault.* New York: Routledge.

Castel, R. (1986) 'Les aventures de la pratique', *Le Débat* 41: 41–51.

Cohen, J. L. (1992) *Le Corbusier and the Mystique of the U. S. S. R.: Theories and Projects for Moscow, 1928–1936.* Princeton: Princeton Architectural Press.

Colomina, B., ed. (1992) *Sexuality and Space.* Princeton, NJ: Princeton University Press.

—— 'Battle Lines: E 1027' (2000) in *Architecturally Speaking,* Read, A., ed. London and New York: Routeledge.

Cotton, N. (2007) 'Made to Measure? Tailoring and the "Normal" Body in Nineteenth-Century France' in *Histories of the Normal and the Abnormal. Social and Cultural Histories of Norm and Normativity,* Ernst, W., ed. London: Routledge.

Cousins, M. and Houssain, A. (1984) *Michel Foucault.* London and New York: Macmillan.

Cousins, M. (1993) 'The First House', transcribed G. Korolija, London. *Arch-Text 1*, 35–8.

—— (1989) 'The practice of historical investigation' in *Post-structuralism and the Question of History*, ed. D. Attridge, G. Bennington and R. Young. Cambridge: Cambridge University Press.

—— 'The Ugly' (2 parts), *AA Files* 28 (1994) 61–4 and *AA Files* 29 (1995) 3–6.

Crary, J. (1992) *Techniques of the Observer.* London and Cambridge, MA: The MIT Press.

Damisch, H. (1995) *The Origin of Perspective*, trans Goodman J. Cambridge, MA and London: The MIT Press.

De Certeau, M. (1984) *The Practice of Everyday Life.* Berkeley and London: University of California Press.

De Landa, M. (1997) *A Thousand Years of Nonlinear History.* New York: Zone Books, The MIT Press.

Deleuze, G. (1969) *Différence et répétition.* Paris: P.U.F.

—— (1969). *Logique du sens.* Paris: Editions de Minuit.

—— (1986) 'La Vie comme une oeuvre d'art', *Le Nouvel Observateur*, 29 August 1986.

—— (2006) *Foucault.* New York: Continuum.

—— and Guattari, F. (1988) *A Thousand Plateaus: Capitalism and Schizophrenia*, trans. B. Massumi. London: The Athlone Press.

Derrida, J. (1986) 'Maintenant l'architecture' in Tschumi, B., *La Case vide.* London: Architectural Association, Folio VIII.

Dreyfus, H. (1982) *Michel Foucault: Beyond Structuralism and Hermeneutics.* Brighton: The Harvester Press.

Dreyfus, H. L. and Rabinow P. (1999/1986) 'What is Maturity? Habermas and Foucault on "What is Enlightenment?"' in *Foucault: A Critical Reader*, ed. D. C. Hoy. Oxford: Blackwell Publishers.

During, S. (1992) *Foucault and Literature.* London: Routledge.

Eisenman, P. (1984) 'The End of the Classical', *Perspecta* 21, 1984, 154–72.

Eribon, D. (1993) *Michel Foucault*, trans. Wing B. London and Boston: Faber and Faber.

Ernst, W. (2007) *Histories of the Normal and the Abnormal. Social and Cultural Histories of Norm and Normativity.* London: Routledge.

Feher, M., Naddaff, R. and Tazi, N., (eds). (1989) *Fragments for the History of Human Body*, vols 1–3. New York: Zone Books.

Flynn, T. (1997) *Sartre, Foucault, and Reason in History: Toward an Existentialist Theory, Vol. 1*. Chicago: University of Chicago Press.

Fontana-Giusti, G. (2011) 'Walling and the city: the effects of walls and walling within the city space', *The Journal of Architecture*, RIBA and Routledge, 16:3, 309–45.

—— (2012) 'The role of small scale images by Wenceslaus Hollar' in *Scale, Imagination, Perception and Practice in Architecture, (*eds). Adler G., Brittain-Catlin T. and Fontana-Giusti G. London and New York: Routledge.

Gerard, D.L. (1998) 'Chiarugi and Pinel considered: Soul's brain/person's mind', *Journal of the History of the Behavioral Sciences*, 33:4, 381–403.

Greenblatt, S. (1980) *Renaissance Self-Fashioning: From More to Shakespeare*. Chicago: University of Chicago Press.

Gregoire, P. (1610) *Syntaxeon artis mirabilis*. Cologne: Lazarus Zetner.

Grosz, E. (1992) 'Bodies/Cities' in *Sexuality and Space*, Colomina, B., ed. Princeton, NJ: Princeton University Press.

Guattari, F. (1972) *Psychanalyse et transversalité. Essais d'analyse institutionnelle*. Paris: F. Maspero.

Guibert, H. (1988) 'Les Secrets d'un homme' in *Mauve le Vierge*. Paris: Gallimard.

Han, B. (2002) *Foucault's Critical project Between the Transcendental and the Historical*, trans. Pile, E. Stanford: Stanford University Press.

Hartley, L. (2007) 'Norms of Beauty and Ugliness in French Culture' in *Histories of the Normal and the Abnormal. Social and Cultural Histories of Norm and Normativity*, ed. Ernst, W. London: Routledge.

Heynen, H. and Baydar G., eds. (2005) *Negotiating Domesticity: Spatial productions of gender in Modern Architecture*. New York and London: Routledge.

Higgins, H. (2009) *The Grid Book*. Cambridge, MA and London: The MIT Press.

Hirst, P. (1992) 'Foucault and Architecture', *AA Files* 26, Autumn, 52–60.

—— (2005) *Space and Power: Politics, War and Architecture*. Cambridge: Polity Press.

Ingraham, C. (1998) *Burdens of Linearity*. London and New Haven: Yale University Press.

Janet, P. (1925) *Psychological Healing: a historical and clinical study*. London: G. Allen & Unwin.

Jardine, A. (1987) 'On bodies and technology' in *Discussions in Contemporary Culture*, ed. H. Foster. Seattle: Bay Press, 151–8.

Korolija Fontana-Giusti, G. (1998) *The Rhetoric of Surfaces and Walls in L.B. Alberti's De commodis litterarum atque in commodis, De picture and De re aedificatoria*. PhD Thesis, University of London.

—— (2000) 'The Cutting Surface: On the Painting as a Section, its Relationship to Writing and its Role in Understanding Space', *AA Files* 40. London: Architectural Association.

Lacan, J. (1987) *The Four Fundamental Concepts of Psychoanalysis*, ed. A. Sheridan. Harmondsworth: Penguin.

Macey, D. (2004) *Michel Foucault*, Critical Lives. London: Reaktion Books.

McCorquodale, D., Wigglesworth S. and Ruedi K., (eds) (1996) *Desiring Practices: Architecture, Gender and the Interdisciplinary*. London: Black Dog Publishing.

McNay, Lois. (1994) *Foucault and Feminism: Power, Gender and the Self*. Oxford: Blackwell Publishers.

Merleau-Ponty, M. (1989) *The Phenomenology of Perception*, trans. C. Smith. London: Routledge.

Middleton, R. (1993) 'Sickness, madness and crime as the grounds of form' parts 1 and 2. *AA-Files* 24 and 25. London: The Architectural Association, 16–31 and 14–30.

Moran, J., Topp, L. and Andrews J., (eds) (2007) *Madness Architecture and Built Environment: Psychiatric spaces in historical context*. London: Routledge.

O'Farrell, C. (2007) *Michel Foucault*. London: Sage.

Peterson, S. K. (1980) 'Space and Anti-Space'. *Harvard Architectural Review* 1, Spring, 88–113.

Pietrowski, A. (2011) *Architecture of Thought*. Minneapolis: The University of Minnesota Press.

Rainbow, P. (1984) *The Foucault Reader*. London: Penguin Books.

Rajchman, J. (1985) *Michel Foucault: The Freedom of Philosophy*. New York: Columbia University Press.

—— (1988) 'Foucault's Art of Seeing', *October 44* (Spring 1988), 88–117.

—— (1998) *Constructions*. London and Cambridge, MA: The MIT Press.

—— (1991) *Truth and Eros, Foucault, Lacan and the Question of Ethics*. London and New York: Routledge.

Schumacher, P. (2010) *The Autopoiesis of Architecture*. London: John Wiley & Sons Ltd.

Semper, G. (1989) *The Four Elements of Architecture and Other Writings*, trans. Harry F. Mallgrave and Wolfgang Herrmann. Cambridge: Cambridge University Press.

Sennett, R. (1994) *Flesh and Stone: The Body and the City In Western Civilization*. New York: Norton.

—— (and Foucault, M. 'Sexuality and Solitude', *London Review of Books* 3:9, 21 May 1981.

Seppä, A. (2004) 'Foucault, Enlightenment and the Aesthetics of the Self', *Contemporary Aesthetics* 2, 1–23.

Shapiro, G. (2003) *Archaeologies of Vision, Foucault and Nietzsche on Seeing and Saying*. Chicago and London: The University of Chicago Press.

Soja, E. (2000) *Postmetropolis, Critical Studies of Cities and Regions*. Oxford: Blackwell Publishers.

Spencer, D. (2011) 'Architectural Deleuzism – Neoliberal Space, Control and the "Univer-City"', *Radical Philosophy* 168 Jul/Aug, 9–21. Charlottesville, VA: Philosophy Documentation Center.

Steinberg, L. (1981) 'Velazquez's "Las Meninas"', *October* 19 (Winter 1981) 45–54.

Still, A. and Irving, V., (eds) (1992) *Rewriting the History of Madness: Studies in Foucault's Histoire de la Folie*. New York: Routledge.

Tafuri, M. (1989) *Venice and the Renaissance*, trans. Levine J. Cambridge, MA and London: The MIT Press.

Trombadori, D. (1999) *Colloqui con Foucault: pensieri, opere, omissioni dell'ultimo maître-à-penser*. Roma: Castelvecchi.

Tschumi, B. (1996) *Architecture and Disjunction*. Cambridge, MA and London: The MIT Press.

Veyne, P. (1979) *Comment on écrit l'histoire suivi de Foucault révolutionne l'histoire*. Paris: Folio/essais.

Vidler, A. (1989) *The Writing of the Walls: Architectural Theory in the Late Enlightenment*. Cambridge, MA and London: The MIT Press.

—— (1994) *The Architectural Uncanny*. Cambridge, MA and London: The MIT Press.

—— ed. (2008) *Architecture between Spectacle and Use*. New Haven and London: Yale University Press.

—— (2011) *The Scenes of the Street and Other Essays*. New York: The Monacelli Press.

West-Pavlov, R. (2009) *Space in Theory, Kristeva, Foucault, Deleuze*. Amsterdam and New York: Rodopi.

Wigley, M. (1992) 'Untitled: The Housing of Gender,' in *Sexuality and Space*, ed. Beatrice Colomina. New York: Princeton Papers on Architecture/ Princeton Architectural Press, 327–89.

—— (1995) *White walls, Designer Dresses: The fashioning of modern architecture*. Cambridge, MA: MIT Press.

Yates, F. (1966) *The Art of Memory*, Ark Editions. London: Routledge.

Zaera-Polo A. and Moussavi F. (2003) *Phylogenesis: FOA's Ark*. Barcelona: Actar.

## Online archives and repositories:

*Repository of texts written by Michel Foucault*, http://foucault.info (accessed 7 October 2012).

*Online Archives*, http://michel-foucault-archives.org/?About-the-Centre-Michel-Foucault (accessed 7 October 2012).

http://www.michel-foucault.com, site maintained by Clare O'Farrell. (accessed 7 October 2012).

http://www.lib.berkeley.edu/MRC/onlinemedia.html, online audio-recording of Foucault's lectures at UC Berkeley April 1983, 'The Culture of the Self' (accessed 7 October 2012).

# Index